The ABCs of
Handwriting
Analysis

The ABCs of Handwriting Analysis

CLAUDE SANTOY

MARLOWE & COMPANY

NEW YORK

Second edition, 1994

Published in the United States by

Marlowe & Company
841 Broadway, Fourth Floor
New York, NY 10003

Distributed by Publishers Group West

Manufactured in the United States of America

Library of Congress Cataloging-in-Publication Data

Santoy, Claude.
    The ABCs of handwriting analysis / Claude Santoy.—1st ed.
        p.   cm.
    ISBN 1-56924-889-3
    1. Graphology.   1. Title.
    BF891.S24 1989   88-22621
    155.2′82—dc19   CIP

Contents

INTRODUCTION

People have been interested in interpreting handwriting for as long as it has been used as a means of communication. As early as the eleventh century in China, Kuo Jo Hsu claimed that, using handwriting, he could distinguish "the noble man from the common man from a moral point of view." In 1662, Camillo Baldo, a Bolognese scholar, published a book entitled *On the Way of Knowing the Nature and Qualities of the Writer by Analysing a Letter Missive.* . . . This treatise, with its laborious title, is more philosophical than scientific.

Graphology has developed considerably since the end of the nineteenth century. The German Johann Caspar Lavater printed several studies concerning the knowledge of human mind through handwriting analysis in his various almanacs. In France, Father Jean Hippolyte Michon successfully rationalized graphology as a science; he and Michel Desbarolles are considered the founders of the Cartesian method, used, in part, to this day. Father Michon published *The Mysteries of Handwriting* in 1869, followed by *The Practical Method.* These books show his keen sense of analysis and observation. In the twentieth century two Swiss men, Max Pulver and John Crepieux-Jamin, devoted themselves to the study of handwriting interpretation and published many books on their discoveries in German and French. Their teaching is by no means out-of-date, although the study of graphology has evolved throughout the world. Their followers include, among others, Ludwig Klages, Robert de Salberg, Ania Teillard and Anne-Marie Cobbaert, as well as the psychiatrists Rene Resten, Paul Joire, and Paul Carton. Medicine and psychoanalysis are helpful complementary studies to graphology. Conversely, handwriting interpretation can help specialists in these fields diagnose the various physical and mental illnesses of their patients; certain cases of mild reactive neuroses can be reduced or even cured with my new method of *graphotherapy*. For example, a depressed person's effort to correct negative aspects in his handwriting may eliminate the corresponding negative character traits. Understand, however, that this new therapy requires the subject's receptivity to be successful. Graphotherapy can also help job-seekers suffering from slight character weaknesses that, although minor, show in their handwriting, preventing them from getting the job they seek.

The use of morphology or chiromancy as complementary studies to graphology is questionable, as is the old typology that classified human temperaments as sanguine, bilious, lymphatic, apathetic, or nervous. People are far more complex, and our characters may well comprise a combination of these traits.

Your handwriting reveals concealed aspects of your character, aspects often inconsistent with your physical appearance and sometimes even with your behavior. It is easier to disguise the meaning of your words than that of your handwriting.

If you appreciate and have studied literature, your experience will help you draw an accurate portrait of your subjects. You need neither be a medium nor a parapsychologist; graphology has nothing to do with the occult. It is a technical procedure, like operations in mathematics.

Nowadays, graphology is being put into practice all over the world. Graphologists, professionals who study handwriting to determine a person's aptitude and character, are employed in various capacities. Companies may routinely ask applicants to send them handwritten resumés for graphologists to interpret. Companies consider this procedure far more profitable than hiring, for example, dishonest certified accountants who will take the money and run. Graphology can help you avoid disappointments in your social and private life. You will know immediately whether or not an acquaintance's character is compatible with yours. Everyone has strong points as well as weak points; humans are not flawless. Nevertheless, it is important to discover whether your partner's specific weaknesses are things you can live with over a long period of time.

The neophyte may ask, what about adventure and the joy of discovery? There is little joy when, for example, a heterosexual woman falls desperately in love with a latently homosexual man whom she persists in pursuing, discovering only months later the immutable truth. Some knowledge of graphology can divert such disappointment and save time for other, more positive love affairs.

A graphologist must not moralize; the meaning of words like "positive" or "negative" must be used flexibly in describing character traits. Any given tendency can have a positive or negative effect, depending on the circumstances and individual. (For example, a diplomatic individual may in fact tell many small lies out of politeness.

If you analyze the letter of a friend whose handwriting betrays both his sensitivity and his tendency to lie, there is no point in openly accusing him and hurting his feelings. Instead, emphasize his business acumen and keen diplomatic skill. You will keep your friend happy while knowing what to expect of him. If he is not too sensitive, you can interpret his mythomania as deviousness. If he is a teenager, you can tell him he has a great imagination.

A graphologist should be both accurate and tactful. If a subject's sample reveals a sexual psychopath with violent tendencies, he should simply be told that he is "very sensuous but somewhat easily angered." It is useless to traumatize a disturbed person with an abrupt analysis that will only confuse him even more. It is dishonest, however, for graphologists to draw completely positive portraits of their clients by overlooking all negative traits.

There is, however, a special difficulty in analyzing the handwriting of children and teenagers and very old people. The former are undergoing great changes, while the latter may be affected by the illnesses and weaknesses that old age is subject to.

For a graphologist, notions of "good" or "bad" handwriting differ from those of an amateur. The latter will often take a regular, embellished and distinguished-looking handwriting for a positive style, although such handwriting, when it is the work of a forty-year old man, for example, may reveal childishness and intellectual deficiency to an experienced graphologist. A regular and monotonous handwriting often reveals mental regression or illness. On the other hand, an irregular and sometimes even jerky writing style may belong to an exceptionally intelligent person, as will be shown.

Avoid tackling the analysis of a renowned person's handwriting in starting out. A genius's handwriting is usually extravagant; his "craziness" is released when he creates. His handwriting style cannot, therefore, be used to reinforce your knowledge of the characteristics most people share.

By following my method, you will learn that a conspicuous good or weak point in handwriting is meaningful, revealing a particular character trait. Both the interplay and the accumulation of signs are crucial. Let us again consider the example of lying. A person can make up harmless lies out of tactfulness; or perhaps the person is a creative writer. In this case the handwriting will be that of a generally honest person. At least four of five specific signs of that particular trait must appear before we can be certain that our candidate lies more often than the average person.

With my new method, you need not know the language in which the sample under analysis was written. Content is not important as long as the sample was written spontaneously. Samples that are copied or dictated show a certain automatism that is likely to distort the analysis. The handwriting of seriously ill people and of children may, however, require a careful reading of the content in order to detect missing words. Nevertheless, usually it is better not to read what the subject has written.

The sample must be written in his mother tongue and from left to right, continuing from the top of the sheet to the bottom. Arabic, Chinese, and Japanese cannot be analyzed with this method.

EQUIPMENT

Ruler.

You will use a ruler to measure the size of the letters, as well as the spacings and the margins. You will also need it to evaluate the basic line of the writing. It can be straight, slightly wavy, or extremely wavy. Even the experienced graphologist uses a ruler, because the evaluation of this basic line is crucial and its appearance can be misleading. Our eyes do not always see the correct picture.

Protractor.

In the beginning you will use a protractor to measure the slant, a crucial point in handwriting analysis. After a few exercises, and certainly by the time you have learned the new method, you will manage without it.

Magnifying glass.

Necessary throughout your career as an amateur or professional graphologist, a magnifying glass will help you detect the less conspicuous aspects of the handwriting before you. A magnifying glass will help you detect evidence of the slightest shaking or trembling of the subject's hand, any unnecessary punctuation, or tiny hidden hooks or retouches otherwise invisible to the naked eye.

HOW TO CHOOSE SAMPLES

Select the handwriting samples of two or three friends. The sample must be written on unlined white paper with either a fountain pen or a ball point pen. Although it is not necessary to read it, the ideal sample is a spontaneous message written to you, expressing the writer's deep feelings and state of mind. A sample of copied text tends to be mechanical. Before you start to analyze the sample, the subject must tell you his age, sex, and profession. A graphologist is neither a solver of riddles nor a medium. When you go to see a doctor, you do not keep your coat on and ask: "Guess where it hurts?" You have to undress. Likewise, sex, age, profession, and education have a crucial influence on one's handwriting. As you continue your study of this book, you will invariably come across some samples similar to those of your friends and will be able to compare character traits. This process will make your study easier, as you will be able to check your discoveries immediately with the person who penned the sample. You will be surprised that your subject will almost always approve your findings.

The following glossary will be useful to you only as a reference, so do not bother to study it thoroughly. I chose to put it at the beginning of my book, to make it convenient for the reader to refer to a technical term or particular sign.

TERMINOLOGY

There are few specific technical terms in graphology. Most of them are self-explanatory; you will not have any trouble remembering their meaning when you encounter them in the following chapters.

In the beginning you will probably refer often to the alphabetical glossary to better understand the exact meaning of each technical term and the corresponding pen strokes. Each term in the glossary is thoroughly explained and illustrated. Several meanings are given; all meanings do not apply to all cases. As will be seen, there is an interplay of signs; their plurality is required in order to discern the real meaning. An isolated sign gives no information. You will need to make the right choice among the possibilities. Little by little, as your knowledge improves through study of this book, your skill will become more acute.

The terminology has applied to most graphological works in all countries, with only few variations, since it was introduced in the beginning of the century by J. Crepieux-Jamin. Some expressions have disappeared as paper and pens have changed. Graphology has adapted to ball point and even to felt pens, although the latter do not allow us to study the pressure, and therefore the health, of the person under analysis.

Altered strokes.

The writer goes back to finished words and tries to improve some of the letters, often without reason; certain letters show a great variety of forms and are often difficult to recognize.

MEANING: Pathological perfectionism; obsessiveness; fear; anxiety; anguish; deceitfulness.

Angular strokes.

Sharp angles prevail.

MEANING: Decisiveness; pragmatism; aggressiveness; virility; materialism; ambition; harshness; selfishness; greed (when accompanied by angular hooks); cruelty; violence. If the pressure is light, the angles mean inner tension and inhibition. The angular writer is irascible and cannot be influenced; he is honest and reliable but difficult to live with. (If hooks, coils, and other negative signs are present, his honesty is questionable.)

Arcades.

Tops of letters are very round; "n" and "m" are printed; arch-like links among letters, words, or other strokes; arches sometimes seen in capital letters.

MEANING: If the writer is under twenty years old and his arcades show only in the "m" and the "n," he is immature and slightly selfish. Otherwise arcades reveal vanity, arrogance, deceitfulness, and manipulativeness.

Backward slant [reversed, *sinistrogyric*].

Handwriting leans towards the left-hand side.

MEANING: Immaturity; egocentricity; stubbornness; incapability in forming deep relationships; often an attachment to mother; obsession with the past; emotional detachment. Subjects are deceitful as friends, are often anxious, and deal with their problems by dissembling and lying.

Baseline.

When you put your ruler underneath a writing sample, you will find that the baseline is straight, slightly meandering, or very meandering.

ascendant
Baseline ascends slightly.

happy disposition

MEANING: Optimism, courage; dynamism.

straight

difficult to influence

MEANING: Reliability; honesty; strong will power; punctuality; principled person.

slightly meandering

a pleasure to meet a

MEANING: Liveliness; intelligence; well-balanced character.

very meandering

that I can be of som you de read me or some

MEANING: Instability; dishonesty; neurosis; tendency to lie.

---

descendant

MEANING: Pessimism; depressive mood; chronic depression; bad physical health.

Clubbed strokes.

Certain strokes become thicker as the pressure increases.

horizontal

MEANING: Emotional detachment; sexual ambivalence that is difficult to repress. Long, clubbed end-stroke reveals a tendency to brutally push friends away in order to preserve personal freedom.

---

vertical

To
Claude Santoy

MEANING: Sexual fantasizing; obsessiveness; inhibitions; frustrations; mental instability; drug or alcohol abuse.

Coils.

These can appear in any letter.

Square

I hope that
I can help

what cartoonish
book I am

MEANING: selfishness; dissimulation; dishonesty. Lying; extreme autoerotism. Slightly coiled—otherwise positive—handwriting indicates good concentration and reasoning power. Business acumen.

Connected script.

Dear Claude Santoy,
Thanks for lending me

MEANING: Analytical and deductive mind; mathematically gifted; good visual memory.

Disconnected [juxtaposed] script.

Brian Hoffman called me
He just got some new drums
marry the woman with the

MEANING: Occasional manual creativity; intuition; independence; good auditory memory; volubility; inner loneliness; great consideration for others.

Disconnected and connected script.

Some letters inside words are connected and some are disconnected.

It seems a pleasant

MEANING: Cultural refinement; intelligence; intellectual
creativity; high ambitions and potential. This kind of writing
is usually speedily done.

Distorted script.

Twisted strokes; use your magnifying glass.

*a change — anyhow I send
and the hope that we will meet*

dedicated

MEANING: Physical and mental suffering; various illnesses.
(See Chapter 2.)

Embellished script.

Dear Claude,
Just a few
to tell you about

Président.

MEANING: Lack of cultural refinement; low intelligence; vanity; selfishness; immaturity; dishonesty.

Forward [progressive] slant.

Handwriting leans towards the right-hand side.

despite the weather though
on which unfortunately
school — you know i can't

passionate.

MEANING: Well-balanced, optimistic person who likes his work. He is dynamic and ambitious, in the positive sense of the word. A very progressive handwriting, as in the second sample, reveals a great passion for all the activities with which the writer is involved. He is sometimes envious and jealous.

Garlands.

The "m" and "n" are written like "u" and "w."

Tiue

MEANING: Friendly, sociable, and adaptable person, easily influenced. Sometimes weak and very stereotypically feminine, if a woman.

NOTE: Every individual has both "masculine" and "feminine" traits (that is, traits that have come to be labelled "masculine" or "feminine" by our society). When we say that a handwriting sample reveals "femininity" or many "masculine" traits, we are referring to these cultural labels. The writer of the sample in question can belong to either sex. Ideally, a well-balanced personality should contain almost equal amounts of "masculine" and "feminine" traits.

Inhibited script.

Backward, regressive slant.

*But I
Before falsifications*

or tight letters with little space between them.

sold without written authority

slightly truncated.

MEANING: Inhibitions; lack of spontaneity; egocentricity. Selfish person who lies and dissimulates. Good concentration.

Jumbled script.

Letters that flow into each other and into other lines.

MEANING: Egocentric and sometimes paranoid personality (depending upon other signs in the writing). Vanity; mental confusion; neurosis; dishonesty.

Launching upward stroke.

Usually appearing at the end of a letter or word, this sign is extremely important. Its meaning applies invariably, even when other confirming signs are absent. It is one of my recent discoveries.

MEANING: The writer has a violent temper, which is difficult for him to keep in check. When he loses his temper, he often screams and becomes aggressive. He can be mean and vengeful.

Loops.

Can be found in consonants; do not confuse with coiling strokes.

MEANING: Tenacity; perseverance; will power; good concentration.

Overlapping strokes.

The writer goes over the same letter twice.

MEANING: Dissimulation; dishonesty; lack of spontaneity.

Pasty script.

Thick, slow, heavy-looking strokes.

> WONDERFUL FRIENDS & NOW
> BE I'LL COME OVER TO VISIT
> YOU ALL! I HOPE THAT YOU ARE
> WELL – NORA IS PREGNANT.
> MUCH LOVE – MaryAnne
>
> girl

MEANING: Indolence; hedonism; tendency to become depressed and neurotic.

Spasmodic script.

Varying pressure within words.

> Australia / All
> the best for 1986

MEANING: Physical or mental illness. Alcohol or drug abuse.

Stick-like script.

most distnguished

Happy

MEANING: The writer has principles, but can be harsh, cruel, selfish, and ruthless. He is callous, hard-working, realistic, and ambitious. (Women seldom write like this.)

Tapered strokes.

smick

tastiau Piu

olga

MEANING: Diplomacy; destructive caustic humor. A regressive libido is indicated in vertical strokes.

Thread letters and connections.

Letters that look like a continuous thread; difficult to distinguish and read.

and speaking French, please call

Ice water   and the

MEANING: With strong pressure of the stroke, the writer has a quick mind and great business acumen. If the pressure is light, the writer can be a liar; he often may suffer from psychosis. Above normal intelligence and intuition.

Unfinished strokes.

Letters that do not reach the baseline.

and in which may
is self-induced

MEANING: The writer is extremely diplomatic; he is often timid, and lies and dissimulates due to inner anxiety and anguish. He is vulnerable, susceptible.

You will encounter many of the terms in this glossary throughout the following chapters. They will be explained again in detail and in connection with specific handwritings. Other samples shall be used to illustrate them: in order to progress in the skill of handwriting analysis it is necessary to study a great number of different samples, so that you can proceed by analogy. Whenever you come across an expression which is not quite familiar to you, don't hesitate to refer to this section.

The ABCs of Handwriting Analysis

I

Elements of Handwriting Analysis

LAYOUT

Apart from the equipment already mentioned, you should now provide yourself with one or two personal letters written on plain, unlined white paper, by people you are especially interested in and whom you do not know well. However, you must know their age, sex, and profession. The handwritten address on the envelope and the signature will also help you with your analysis. Keep these documents beside the book so that you may immediately put into practice whatever you learn. Jot down possible meanings of your friends' samples as you study this section.

Margins.

The interpretation of margins, although easy, is not absolute and must blend with other discoveries.

paragraphs
The first written line of each paragraph indents a few spaces inside the alignment of the left margin.

MEANING: Sense of order; good social integration; spontaneity. Paragraphs in which every line is aligned mean the writer is slightly inhibited and shy.

---

left margin

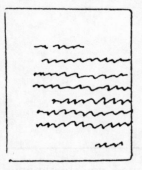

Large and regular: A clear mind; consideration for others; good education; organization; generosity (if other signs confirm it).

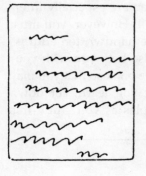

Decreasing towards the bottom: Pessimism; caution; fear; weakness; depression.

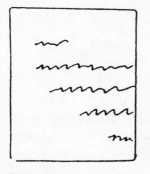

Increasing towards the bottom: Spontaneity; independence; carelessness. The writer is easily influenced.

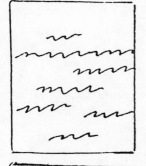

Irregular: Instability; limited reliability.

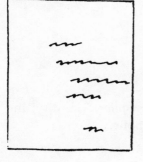

Very large: Neurosis; psychosis. The writer always strives for the future through work or excessive activity, which can turn into agitation and restlessness.

right margin

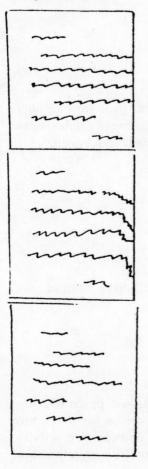

Narrow or absent: Adaptability; well-balanced character; sound judgment; vitality.

Absent with downward slopes: Reck-lessness; impatience; selfishness; vol-ubility; immoderation.

Very large or irregular: Timidity; in-stability; inhibitions.

top margin

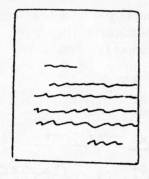

Large: Great consideration for others; humility.

(*Too large:* inhibition; timidity.)

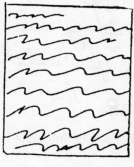

Narrow: Selfishness; arrogance; avariciousness; immaturity.

NOTE: Absence of margins (the whole paper is filled with writing): bad judgment; selfishness; lavishness; intrusive personality seeking protection; immaturity; neurosis.

Spacing.

When you examine a handwriting sample you have to consider the spacing between lines, words, and letters. The following samples will help you perceive differences between various spacings and what they mean.

regular spaces between lines and words

> It occurs to me that
> might be locating copies
> oby's novels as you
> to England. Would
> able / willing to

MEANING: Well-balanced, organized, socially integrated, and relatively happy person.

large spaces between lines and words

> n hair   I see you
> 1 day   and   dream
> how   it   could   be.....
> is   the   secret   of   that

MEANING: Independence; idealism; isolation; hedonism.

narrow spaces between lines and words,
Sometimes in jumbled handwriting.

MEANING: The writer is dependent on others to the point of neurosis; often confused, he cannot make decisions because he feels helpless. He suffers anguish and tends to be phobic.

irregular spaces between lines and words

fmale`. Just met a very old
schoolfriend in the street right
around the corner, funnyhow
Paris seems to attract people like
a magnet. Must go now!

MEANING: Instability; inconstant loyalty; changeable moods; immaturity, credulousness; neurosis.

---

illogical spaces between letters within words

which I am myself involved
emanuel person, be essentles

years old – NO – you
s all the next week
have the –

MEANING: Psychosis; schizophrenia; deficient nervous system; deviated emotions; split personality.

NOTE: "Deviated emotions" is a technical term used in psychoanalysis. If, for instance, someone experiences a happy event, instead of being pleased, he will break into tears and become worried. He may feel guilty for crimes he has not commited or commit crimes and not feel guilty. In short, the person's emotions do not "match" his external circumstances.

Envelope Addresses.

The position of the address also gives some clues to the writer's personality. First, compare the handwriting in the letter with that on the envelope. They must have the same aspect. If they look very different, the person dissimulates and lies. He is not trustworthy.

Now let's examine the various positions of the address and what they mean. It is, however, necessary to check the custom of the country if the letter is sent from someone overseas. In the USSR, for example, the address is normally written on the upper left-hand side of the envelope.

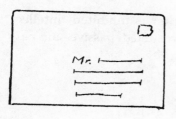

Intelligent, well-educated, spontaneous person.

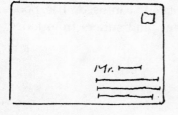

The writer is pragmatic, materialistic, ambitious, rather selfish, and efficient in his work.

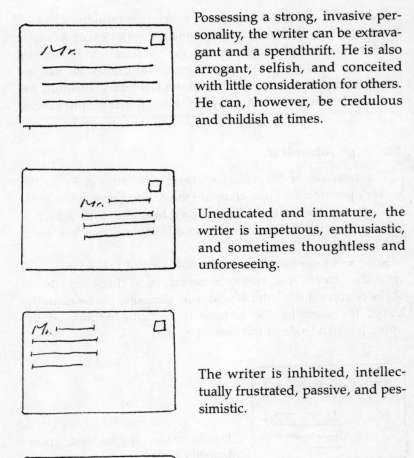

Possessing a strong, invasive personality, the writer can be extravagant and a spendthrift. He is also arrogant, selfish, and conceited with little consideration for others. He can, however, be credulous and childish at times.

Uneducated and immature, the writer is impetuous, enthusiastic, and sometimes thoughtless and unforeseeing.

The writer is inhibited, intellectually frustrated, passive, and pessimistic.

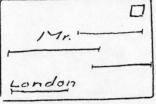

The writer is pathologically unstable, isolated, confused, has poor judgment, and suffers from loneliness.

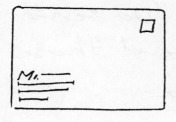

The writer is sexually inhibited, submissive, timid, with a tendency towards envy and vindictiveness.

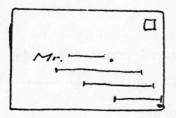

This address, resembling a staircase, indicates that the writer does not trust others; he dissimulates and lies. If a full stop or any unnecessary dot follows the address, the meaning is intensified.

Signatures.

The analysis of the signature is part of the study of the whole letter. A letter with no signature gives us less insight into the writer's personality. Likewise, a signature alone is not sufficient to draw a clear, precise portrait. The latter demands the analysis of a whole page of spontaneous writing with a signature at the end and, if possible, a handwritten address on the envelope.

Let's examine the signature and its relationship to the letter's text.

The signature is placed towards the right-hand side at a certain interval underneath the text. The signature looks similar to the handwriting in the text and is easy to read. There is no paraph underneath.

doesn't it? Do send
us, as I send those
to you Anne,
Darren

MEANING: Intelligent, well-balanced, honest, and reliable person.

The signature is placed far from the text.

The electricity money
job and every thing works

Noël

MEANING: The writer feels isolated, inhibited, and frustrated.

The signature is placed too close to the text.

visionary of the distortion. Amen. A love Jon

MEANING: Neurotic attachment to others; the writer feels insecure, anxious, and inferior. He or she may possess psychotic tendencies, if confirmed by other signs.

The signature is placed in the middle or towards the left-hand side.

the sentence with your medium pen.

David E. Retcker

MEANING: Inhibitions; depression; neurosis; pessimism; no self-confidence.

The handwriting in the text ascends and the signature descends.

MEANING: The writer has high goals but is incapable of achieving them; physical and mental exhaustion.

The initial letters bend towards the left-hand side, and are followed by straight or progressive letters.

MEANING: The writer is still attached to his parents and suffers from past family conflicts.

The initial letters are high and narrow.

MEANING: The writer is vain due to a profound feeling of inferiority, selfishness, arrogance.

The signature is smaller than the handwriting in the text.

first trip

to veer

Sherry

MEANING: The writer feels isolated and socially ill at ease; he suffers from psychological complexes and inhibitions. He is not confident. He usually associates with people less well-educated than he is in order to be at ease. The humility of the writer is excessive and sometimes neurotic.

The baseline of the signature ascends while the text is straight.

Amsterdam! Happy Holidays and so on!

Love Seker

MEANING: The goals of the writer transcend his ability to achieve them. He lacks good judgment.

The baseline is meandering.

MEANING: Instability; unreliability; the person is diplomatic and will lie if necessary.

The signature differs greatly from the handwriting of the text and address. (If the writer is a businessperson, doctor, or anyone who signs many letters a day, the following meaning does not apply.)

like again.

See ya

MEANING: The writer is untrustworthy; he lies and dissimulates.

The signature is surrounded by a paraph.

MEANING: The writer is attached to his belongings; he can be possessive, but takes care of his family.

Vertical strokes or paraphs in the signature.

MEANING: The writer is pragmatic and can be ruthless, selfish, and materialistic.

The signature is followed by a dot or a full stop.

MEANING: The writer hardly ever trusts anyone and is usually lying.

The signature is crossed out by its paraph, which is often angular.

MEANING: The angles reveal vengefulness, and the paraph that crosses the signature shows the writer's destructive and often self-destructive tendencies.

NOTE: A wide and garlanded signature belongs to a friendly, generous, and sociable person. A narrow and angular signature reveals the writer to be tough, ambitious, selfish, reliable, difficult to influence, and materialistic. The signature analysis follows, in general, the guidelines used to interpret other handwriting, as you will see in following chapters. Remember that the most positive signature is one that matches in every aspect the handwriting of the address and the text. Bankers agree that a simple, readable signature is far more difficult to imitate than an embellished one.

SIZE

This sketch-plan of the three principal zones can be applied generally, even to doodles and drawings.

upper zone		upper loops upper stems	*meaning:* Intellectual ambitions; ideals; mysticism; dreams; imagination.
middle zone			*meaning:* Realism; living in the present; materialism; hedonism.
lower zone		lower loops lower sticks	*meaning:* Sexuality; pragmatism; physical movement; enjoys sports.

The meaning of the slant is shown below.

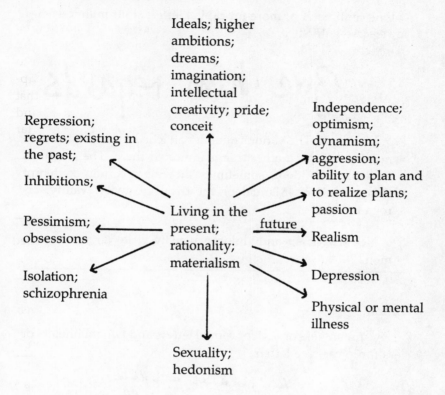

Ideals; higher ambitions; dreams; imagination; intellectual creativity; pride; conceit

Repression; regrets; existing in the past;

Inhibitions;

Pessimism; obsessions

Isolation; schizophrenia

Living in the present; rationality; materialism

future

Independence; optimism; dynamism; aggression; ability to plan and to realize plans; passion

Realism

Depression

Physical or mental illness

Sexuality; hedonism

This sketch-plan is easily applied to the size of the handwriting, as you will see in the following samples. You will also refer to it when you study the different slants and their meanings.

As you study this section, jot down some possible meanings, as regards size, as they pertain to your friends' samples.

Large.

One centimeter or more for capital letters, four milimeters for lower-case letters.

Give him regards

MEANING: The various qualities attached to large handwriting depend upon other things indicated there. The person is generally confident, sometimes showing a certain contempt towards others. Manual or theatrical creativity; vanity; arrogance.

NOTE: Women and children usually write larger than do men.

Small.

Five milimeters or less for capital letters and two milimeters or less for lower-case letters.

Rin, maybe a place to stay there. I'll

MEANING: If written fast it belongs to an intelligent, well educated person, and usually indicates virility. Here, too, all depends on the slant, pressure, and other signs.

Average.

Between five milimeters and one centimeter for capital letters, between two milimeters and four centimeters for lower-case letters.

Looking

MEANING: A well-balanced personality if no negative signs are present, such as backward slant, coils or hooks.

Exaggerated.

too small

*I am you gamma with is not so good
Hower ... to go*

MEANING: The person is mean, greedy, selfish, deceitful and lacks self-confidence.

too large

I do go

MEANING: Egocentric, conceited, and selfish character. Megalomania; psychosis.

letters spread out mainly in the middle zone.

see you when you are

MEANING: Materialism; manual skill; attachment to others; hedonism; profligacy; sometimes indolence, depending on the general aspect. In this case, strong pressure indicates an affectionate personality.

long stems or loops

delightful

affect ones

MEANING: Ambitions and frustrations. High stems and punctuation indicate vanity, imagination, and intellectual creativity. Plunging loops indicate strong libido.

SLANT

As you have no doubt gathered by reading the glossary, the notion of the slant is crucial. The sketch-plan that illustrates the meaning of size will also help in your study of the meaning of the different slants. Your protractor and magnifying glass will prove useful.

Remember that the slant of teenagers' and children's handwriting does not have the same meaning as that of adults—let's say people over twenty years old. Youngsters between thirteen and seventeen years old quite often produce a backward slant. The meaning is not necessarily negative in their case.

Measure the slant in your friends' samples, adding possible meanings to those you have noted on layout and size. You will be able to make the synthesis at the end of the first chapter.

The slant is not always as obvious as suggested in the glossary. Further study of samples will help your progress.

Forward [progressive] slant.

only to say yes and
t us sleep together
aps Sunday night?

MEANING: Ambition; enthusiasm; spontaneity; optimism.

Very forward slant.

I'm sure shell be
to school will be
much for all you

MEANING: The writer is passionate about his work and hobbies; he can be jealous.

Upright script.

No particular slant.

had really not altered
Anny (except for om
I a court and a caster

are sorry about not
you from Barcelona

MEANING: The writer has good concentration, is realistic, but lacks spontaneity. He is reflective and ruled by reason.

Backward slant.

It can range from slightly to extremely backward.

professional
At my last stop
I had the chance

MEANING: The writer is more or less inhibited, egocentric, apathetic, distrustful, afraid of the future, selfish, and capable of lying in order to hide all these negative traits. His concentration is good when he does not lavish it on himself or the past. Great stubbornness.

Varying slants in the same sample or in different samples written by the same person.

Use your magnifying glass; these differences can be very slight.

MEANING: Instability; imbalance; indecision; neurosis; anxiety; cyclic moods. The writer is immature and untrustworthy, and is susceptible to schizophrenia or drug addiction (check other signs in his writing).

Forward slant with backward strokes.

creatif

Sylvia Beech first published it.
tended to stay the night here
get a hold of my friends
I stayed one night, I got hold
nds, but still stayed here because
here.

MEANING: The writer is ambitious, vengeful, and able to dissimulate and lie. Exception: If these backward strokes are loops, simply indicate perseverance.

Slant of the baseline.

straight

Use your ruler.

Shakespeare & Company

MEANING: The writer is principled, strong-willed, hardworking, punctual, pragmatic, reasonable, trustworthy, well-balanced, and sometimes stubborn.

---

slightly meandering

I would chive you where ever you

MEANING: Intelligence, wit, good education, quick mind.

very meandering

consider me for your

help me out and would

were expected

MEANING: Instability.

NOTE: If a slightly meandering baseline is a positive sign, a very meandering baseline is, on the contrary, a negative sign.

descendant

as are different things as well - looking
is a possible college for my son save
my feeling - but he liked it.
to say Vassar i. at.

MEANING: Depression, precarious health, neurosis, psychosis.

ascendant

MEANING: Optimism, ambition, good health, high goals, dynamism; hysterics.

_____ SPEED _____

It is important to establish whether a person writes slowly or speedily. Some indication concerning his culture, intelligence, spontaneity, patience, disposition, vivacity of mind, and, sometimes, his integrity can be discovered.

However, speed by itself has little meaning; as with all other signs, it has to be considered with other observations. The number, interplay, and recurrence of signs must be taken into account before making the final synthesis.

There are two ways to evaluate speed. The easiest is watching the person write; if this is not possible, remember that a fairly clear, readable handwriting with a progressive slant and a normal to light pressure can be considered speedy. A connected garlanded stroke indicates even greater speed. Slow handwriting may be embellished, altered, very angular, or have a backward slant. In a straight or progressive slant you may find hooks, disconnected script, or reversed strokes that slow the speed, as well as pasty, heavy pressure.

Once you have established the speed of a given sample, keep in mind the following: in a speedy handwriting each positive factor intensifies in meaning, and in a slow handwriting the same is true of the defects.

There are exceptions. An artist who is close to genius, or a manual worker who rarely uses a pen is liable to write either slowly or, on the contrary, extremely fast, including hooks or backward strokes. The graphologist has to make allowances in these cases. To repeat, it is useless to study samples from famous people when learning handwriting; their artistic skill provides outlets for their negative personality traits. Thus, remember to ask for the subject's profession or educational background.

Speedy and positive.

Slow and negative.

awoke I had no idea of where
omit abit, it took me a good
finally remembered and felt
I assured at Shakespeare

gorating and always
I wouldn't mind

_____ **PRESSURE** _____

Experience in examining various handwriting samples is necessary in order to appraise pressure. It is, of course, extremely difficult to analyze a photocopy or a sample written in pencil or with a felt pen, so concentrate on spontaneous letters written with a fountain pen or ball point.

First, hold the sample upside down towards the light. If bulging lines appear, the pressure is heavy. If they don't and you can just barely guess there is writing on the other side, the pressure is light.

The pressure helps you discover:

1. mental and physical health

2. libido (which includes joy in living, will power, and sexuality)

3. energy and vivacity

4. balance and adaptability

5. sensuality and affection

6. aggression

7. apathy

Heavy.

all about. A day
relished the
we are born to.

MEANING: Good health; well-balanced personality; decisiveness; responsibility; ambition; energy; will power; selfishness; strong libido; affectionate nature.

Light.

handwriting is good!
short years here I've
ed that I've come and

MEANING: Precarious health; cultural refinement; intelligence; sensitivity; romantic sensibilities. The writer is sociable and generous, easily influenced, restless, irritable, and nervous. Quick and sharp-minded, he can possess intellectual creativity. His libido is often weak, sometimes there is latent neurosis. Be sure to make the right choices among these possibilities.

Clubbed or irregular.

Some strokes are thicker than others; variable pressure.

profunde affection

this morning , ' am

now booked for

MEANING: Bad health; severe restlessness; instability; lack of control; deviated emotions; frequently, sexual ambivalence; frustrations difficult to bear; neurosis; psychosis; schizophrenia; limited reliability; chronic illness; sometimes alcohol or drug addiction.

SHAPE

In the glossary you have seen samples, with their meanings, of a number of shapes that occur in handwriting. Here follows a more thorough summary; later there will be further explanation of each letter in the alphabet.

As with the other factors, shape alone has very little meaning. As you know, the cumulative interplay of the given pressure, size, speed and spacing must be considered. To undertake a serious analysis, it is necessary to have more than one or two handwritten words at your disposal. Usually a few lines or a short spontaneous letter are sufficient as shown in the "Practical Analysis" section.

A handwriting is round when the overall impression is one of roundness. The same principle applies to all the other shapes mentioned below. In some cases you will need your magnifying glass to discern details.

Presented are several samples illustrating each shape. A number of possible meanings are proposed for each. All of them do not apply; it is up to you to make the right choice by taking other elements into account, such as the slant, the envelope, and the signature. Little by little your skill will improve and it will become easy for you to trace a precise portrait of the writer who submitted his sample to you.

Round.

you, but I'm very
bar job is O.K., but
I drink too much.

she can't clean
very happy to see
you are only a

milling   around

I Feel   sort of

apartment near
introduced to
houseboy.

MEANING: The writer is friendly, sociable, affectionate, traditionally feminine, easily influenced, adaptable; attached to pleasures, and the money necessary to obtain them. She can be selfish, sometimes using charm to manipulate others.

Angular.

a profound probe into
the Sahara by bus, then
truck, then donkey, then
down on all fours! I want

I will try to get the key
sometime this week...

MEANING: The writer is ambitious, hard-working, dynamic, realistic, materialistic, principled and trustworthy. He can, however, be ruthless, tough, and selfish. He usually achieves his aims. His personality is stereotypically masculine. Regressive angles mean the writer is vengeful and often nasty. Angular hooks on the ends of or inside letters reveal greed, which causes him to lie.

Mixture of round and angular.

I have been informed

I am privileged to have

occasionally, carrots

nutritional poverty of

quite clearly a

Please say hello

to Philippe for

MEANING: A well-balanced person with an analytical and deductive mind; he is intelligent and well-educated. He is open to new suggestions and capable of adapting himself to unexpected situations.

Garlands.

and then I have my

to sit down and spontaneous letter

experience

correspondance

national

formation

MEANING: The writer is extremely friendly, sociable, and diplomatic, and strives to achieve his aims through charm and seduction. He can integrate himself into any society and situation. He is hedonistic, unprincipled sometimes, and easily influenced. Often his character is rather weak, lacking determination and decisiveness.

Thread letters and connections.

MEANING: His business acumen is well-developed, if the pressure is strong. Extremely diplomatic, the writer can lie if he thinks it necessary.

However, if the pressure is light and the baseline meandering, the person fibs and lies from anxiety. Unstable and often unbalanced, he tends towards psychosis; tries to escape reality.

Jarring, altered, and jumbled.

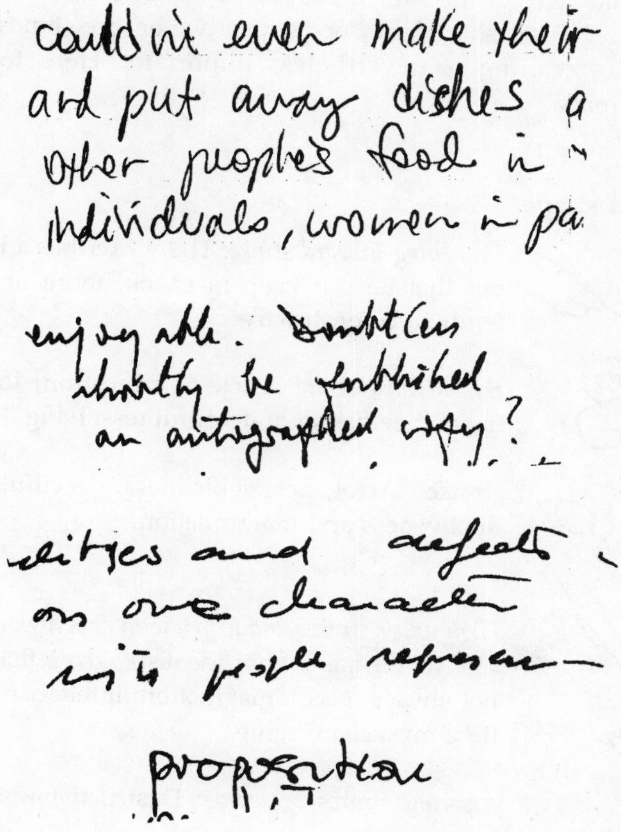

[handwritten text samples]

MEANING: The writer is not well-balanced; he may lack intelligence and education. He is capable of lying and stealing. He suffers from numerous neuroses or psychoses that he tries to hide. Anxiety; anguish.

Along with the above summary of principal shapes, you should refer to the sketch-plan of size and to the terminology section. Some shapes may occur only two or three times a page. Their meaning is nevertheless important. Here follows a summary.

Odd shapes.

Launching upward stroke: The writer has a bad temper that he can keep in check, more or less; he tends to be destructive.

Embellished script: Lack of education; low intelligence; selfishness; deceitfulness; lying.

Arcades: Arrogance; selfishness; deceitfulness; seductiveness and manipulation.

High upper strokes and loops, with dots high on the "i": The writer has higher idealistic goals that he cannot always reach; imagination; intellectual frustration; mysticism; vanity.

Tapering strokes or words: Destructiveness; caustic humor.

Larger letters towards the end of a word: Gullibility.

Very long strokes and stems that extend below the lower zone: The writer is pragmatic, materialistic, and sexually and materialistically frustrated.

Inflated upper loops: The writer is romantic, hoping to find an ideal love. Gullibility; tendencies toward "feminine" qualities.

Inflated lower loops: Unfulfilled sexual fantasies; unsatisfied sexual life. In men the inflated loops show sexual ambivalence (homosexual and bisexual tendencies).

Horizontal clubbed strokes: In men, homosexual and bisexual tendencies.

Stick-like script: The writer is tough, ruthless, and sometimes nasty. If a woman, this indicates "masculine" qualities.

This section concerning the shape is slightly longer than the preceding sections, because we are giving the shape and meaning of each letter of the alphabet. However, you must not forget that the shape of only one letter is of very little meaning; consider the cumulative interplay of all strokes and the general aspect of the writing.

—————— Alphabet ——————

Simplified: Well-balanced and educated person.

Knotted loop: Perseverance; diligence.

High and narrow: Vanity; inferiority complex.

Small and narrow:
Timidity;
inhibition.

Concave stroke:
Sense of humor;
wit; optimism.

Uncrossed:
Carelessness;
arrogance

Embellished: Lack of
education; vanity;
low intelligence;
stupidity;
selfishness; lying.

Very small: Neurotic
inferiority complex;
inhibition.

Overlapping strokes:
Dissimulation;
diplomacy; anxiety;
lying

Backward angular stroke:
Vengefulness; aggressiveness;
nastiness.

*Unfinished stroke that doesn't reach
the baseline:* The writer is
vulnerable, sensitive, capable of
lying, susceptible (easily hurt).

Stroke reaching below the baseline: The
writer is pragmatic and materialistic,
and can be ruthless.

Simplified: Well-balanced and educated person.

Open at the top: Sociable; voluble personality.

Ringlets: The writer is charming, seductive, "feminine."

Coiled: Dissimulation; selfishness; lying, extreme autoerotism.

Coiled stroke on top: Greed; selfishness; business acumen.

Very large: Gullibility.

Script-like: Literary aims and creativity.

Clockwise stroke, usually open at the bottom: Untrustworthy, the writer can lie and steal, is greedy, selfish, and unprincipled.

Very open at the top: The writer is indiscreet, talkative, and can be slanderous. Incapable of keeping a secret.

Disconnected strokes: Split personality; neurosis.

Filled with ink: Fantasies of sexual debauchery.

Variety of shapes of the same letter by the same writer; sometimes altered and difficult to recognize: Weak, neurotic person who lies.

Simplified: Well-balanced and educated person.

High: Vanity.

Embellished or coiled: lack of education and intelligence; greed; selfishness; hypocrisy; lying.

Disconnected strokes: Split personality; neurotic tendencies.

Very high and narrow: Inferiority complex due to past poverty.

Simplified: Education; intelligence; respect for others.

Schoolish (resembles writing of a school-aged child who has just learned penmanship; devoid of individual character): Well-balanced, slightly stubborn person.

Concave beginning stroke: Sense of humor; wit; optimism.

Knotted loop at the end: Perseverance.

High, narrow upper loop: High goals and idealism, and frustration concerning these aims.

Coiled or overlapping strokes: Business acumen; dissimulation; diplomacy; lying; selfishness; narcissism.

Open at the bottom or disconnected strokes: Neurotic tendencies.

Wide middle zone: The writer is friendly, affectionate, materialistic, and hedonistic, with manual ability and creativity.

Simplified: Intelligent, well-balanced person.

Coiled: Greed; lying; business acumen.

Large and round: Generosity; affection; sensuality.

Simplified: Great intelligence; quick mind; wit; good education; intellectual creativity; intuition.

Coiled: Greed; narcissism; selfishness; lying.

Simplified: Well-balanced and educated person.

Open on top: Sociability.

Open at the bottom: Hypocritical person who likes to spread rumors.

Knotted loops: Perseverance; good concentration.

Disconnected strokes: Split personality.

Coiled: Greed; lying; business acumen.

Simplified: Well-balanced and educated person.

Backward stroke in the stem: The writer lives in the past, is inhibited, dissimulates, and lies. Business acumen.
Since this was the normal way of writing a "d" at the beginning of the twentieth century, do not apply the above meaning to older people.

Open at the bottom: Deceit; hypocrisy; dishonesty. The person might steal if given the opportunity.

High stem: Vanity; mysticism; high, idealistic aims that the person cannot reach, and resultant frustration.

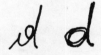

Narrow: Neurosis; the writer suffered from money problems or poverty in the past.

Coiled or overlapping strokes: Capacity to concentrate, dissimulate, and lie. Business acumen; narcissism; extreme autoerotism; selfishness.

Progressive, launching upward stroke: Choleric, quick-tempered person.

Disconnected strokes: Neurotic tendencies.

Very round in the middle: Hedonism; gluttony; very affectionate personality.

Over-simplified, altered: Quick mind; intuition; impatience.

Small hook (examine with your magnifying glass): Greed; deceit; lying.

Simplified: Well-balanced and educated person.

Coiled: Materialism; selfishness; business acumen.

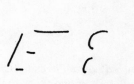

Disconnected or uneven strokes: Neurosis.

High and narrow: Inhibitions; vanity.

Simplified: Well-balanced and educated person.

Unfinished, suspended stroke: The person is vulnerable, inhibited, timid, impatient, and sometimes neurotic.

Short end-stroke: The writer is mean and very selfish.

Concave ending: Generosity; friendliness; sociability.

Regressive end-stroke, hooks: Greed; egotism.

Tapered ending (examine with your magnifying glass.) Destructiveness; violence; caustic humor.

Pasty: Dreams of debauchery; sexual perversion; weak heart and health problems.

Variety of shapes of the same letter by the same writer: Carelessness; no respect for others; deceit; lying; anxiety; neurosis.

Ending stroke reaches below the baseline: Materialistic and sexual ambitions, and frustration in these areas. Pessimism.

Clubbed horizontal end-stroke: Deviated emotions; sexual ambivalence.

Simplified: Well-balanced and educated person.

Similar to the lower-case form: Fatalistic or pessimistic attitude; weak libido.

Embellished or overlapping strokes: Hypocrisy; anxiety; dishonesty; vanity; stupidity; selfishness; neurosis.

Script-like: Intelligent and well-educated, the writer can be tough and very materialistic.

Loops crossing in the middle are of normal length: Well-balanced person with a strong libido.

Knotted loop on the baseline: Perseverance; will power.

High stem: Idealistic and mystical goals that are difficult to achieve, with resultant frustration; vanity; inferiority complex.

Short upper stem with long lower loop: Materialistic and sexual ambitions, and frustration in these areas.

Inflated upper loop: Dreaminess; romantic personality; inhibitions.

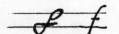

Short upper and lower stems:
Materialism, with no other
ambitions. The person lives in
the present, is affectionate,
hedonistic. Usually has a
manual bent.

*High upper stem with a long lower
loop or stick-like stroke:*
Intellectual and sexual
ambitions and frustrations.

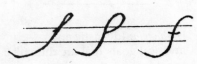

*Open lower loop turned backward,
sometimes with a sharp tapered
ending:* The writer has
inhibitions and is unsatisfied
sexually and is resentful. Selfish
and cunning, he suffers from
deviated emotions. He can be
depraved, has destructive tendencies, and is nonchalant.

Low crossing in a simplified letter:
The person tries to repress or
avoid sexual or materialistic
impulses. Asceticism.

Concave initial stroke: Good
sense of humor; optimism.

Regressive angle in the lower loop:
The person is resentful,
vengeful, envious, and can
become nasty and aggressive.

Beginning stroke is long: The writer has a critical mind, and is cautious and sensible.

Twisted, weak, and altered shapes and disconnected strokes: Physical and psychological suffering; bad health; weakened libido; bisexual or homosexual tendencies.

Simplified: Well-balanced and educated person.

Coiled: Selfishness; business acumen; lying; materialism.

Regressive angles in the lower part: The writer is resentful, vengeful, and envious, and suffers from entrenched and unconquerable sexual inhibitions.

Similar to number 8: Intellectual creativity; sexual ambivalence; anguish; mental problems.

Altered, difficult to recognize: Quick mind; impatience; lying; dishonesty.

Large and round: The writer needs lots of affection. Femininity; generosity.

Simplified: Honest, well-educated, and well-balanced person with some latent manual creativity.

Long lower loop: Strong libido; dynamism.

Very long lower stroke or loop. Very strong libido. Frustrated sexual and material ambitions.

Open lower loop: Unsatisfactory sex life.

No lower loop, tapered stroke: Regressed libido; indolence.

Pronounced, inflated middle with open or reduced lower loop or stroke: Resentful, ambivalent person.

Vertical clubbed stroke or loop: Sexual fantasies; obsessions and inhibitions; drug abuse.

Various twisted shapes: Sexual ambivalence and perversions.

Inflated lower loop that can reach into line below: Sexual fantasies; the writer needs to move and participate in sports.

Tapered regressive and open loop of the lower zone: Destructive and self-destructive tendencies; unsatisfactory sex life.

Simplified: Well-balanced and educated person; honesty.

Narrow: Timid, fearful, and critical person who does not trust anyone.

Knotted loop: Perseverance; tenacity.

Wide: Profligacy; generosity; friendliness.

Simplified: Well-educated person.

High loop overreaching the upper zone: High goals, frustration concerning professional achievement; vanity; neurosis.

Unfinished, suspended strokes:
Diplomacy; inhibition;
sensitivity; vulnerability;
timidity; lying.

Inflated upper loop: Mysticism;
dreamy; "feminine" personality.

Coiling: Business acumen;
materialism; selfishness; greed.

Long, tapering beginning stroke:
Critical mind. The writer is
observant and careful in his
actions.

Simplified: Well-balanced and
educated person.

Hooks or Coils: Greed; lack of
education and intelligence;
lying.

Simplified with dot above: Well-
balanced and educated person.

Dot above and to the right:
Optimism; ambition; joy in
living; dynamism.

Dot above and to the left: Inhibited, depressed, and weak person who lives in the past.

Thick heavy dot: Materialism; cynism; neurotic tendencies.

No dot: Indolence; selfishness; lack of consideration for others; carelessness.

Dot placed low, near the stem: Realistic, materialistic personality.

Dot placed high above: Imagination; high goals.

Dot like a circle: Immaturity; childishness.

Dot like a hook: Greed.

Dot connected to the following letter: Analytical and mathematical skill; vivacity; intelligence.

Simplified: Well-balanced and educated person.

Coiled: Business acumen; selfishness; lying.

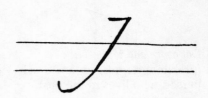

Embellished: Lack of intelligence; lying; deceit, hypocrisy.

Starting or finishing below the baseline: Selfishness; materialism; depression; lying.

Simplified: Well-balanced and educated person.

Long initial stroke: Critical, analytical mind. The person is careful and circumspect in business—never impulsive.

Open loop in the lower zone: Unsatisfactory sex life.

Inflated, tapered open loop: Destructive, ambivalent, vindictive character. Repressed violence; neurosis; deceit.

Angles: Sexual disappointment and resentment.

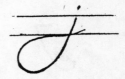

Inflated, closed loop: Sexual fantasies; sexual ambivalence.

Very long loop: Materialism; sexual ambition; frustration; strong libido.

Stick-like: Selfishness; harshness; materialistic ambition.

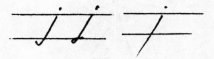

Dot high above: Imagination.

Short or tapered stem; Weak, regressive libido; little interest in sex; precarious health; indolence.

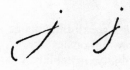

Twisted strokes: Physical and mental suffering; perversion; sexual ambivalence; disease.

Frail or broken stroke: Heart ailment; high blood pressure; disease.

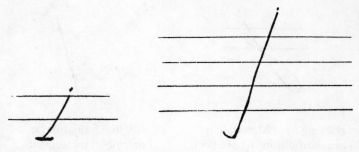

Horizontal stroke in the lower stem: Asceticism; masochism.

Very long stem without loop: Selfishness; hypocrisy.

Simplified: Well-balanced and educated person.

Knotted loop: Tenacity.

Unfinished stroke: Impatience; ambition; diplomacy; vulnerability; irritability.

Disconnected strokes: Intuition; imagination; split personality.

Resembling the letter "X": Complicated personality; aggressive and nasty behavior towards others.

Embellished: Hypocrisy; lack of intelligence.

Simplified: Well-balanced and educated person.

High stem: Vanity; intellectual ambition and frustration.

Inflated upper loop: Chimerical dreams; theatrical creativity; friendliness; femininity.

Coiled: Business acumen; greed; dishonesty; lack of education.

Simplified: Well-educated person.

Knotted loops: Tenacity; perseverance; gentleness.

Embellished: Hypocrisy; cunning.

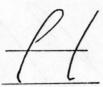

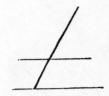

Simplified: Well-balanced, educated person.

Stick-like: Materialistic, selfish, and harsh character; intuition.

High stem: Vanity; ambitions higher than the capability of the writer.

Angular: Pragmatic, principled person who can be trusted. Angles in the upper part mean that the person is resentful and nasty.

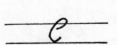

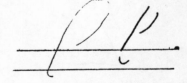

Mainly situated in the middle: Manual or technical creativity; hedonism; no intellectual or cultural pursuits; materialism.

Broken or twisted stem: Precarious health; high blood pressure; physical suffering; dysfunctional thyroid.

Simplified: Intelligent, well-educated person.

High initial stroke: Vanity; irritability; sensitivity; megalomania.

Superfluous strokes: Deviated emotions; neurosis.

High end-stroke: Envy; inferiority complex; glory-seeking; vanity; superficiality; choleric temper.

Long end-stroke: Violence; brutality; materialistic pursuits; selfishness; difficult character; latent neurosis; tendency to contradict others.

Arcades: Manipulative personality; diplomacy; false friendliness; stubbornness; discretion; selfishness; hypocrisy.

Garlanded: The writer is adaptable, friendly, gentle, affectionate, and easily influenced.

Disconnected: Intuition; split personality.

High and narrow: Inferiority complex; vanity.

Large, spread-out: Generosity; profligacy.

Mixture of garlanded and angular script: Well-balanced and educated person.

Garlanded or garlands with ringlets: "Feminine" qualities; charm; friendliness; seductive power; adaptability; sociability. The writer can, however, be easily influenced, weak, and indolent.

Arcades: Stubbornness; immaturity; insincerity; arrogance. The writer knows how to manipulate others, is selfish, often hypocritical, and may lie.

Thread-like: The writer is intelligent, irritable, impatient, and diplomatic; he has a quick mind and can lie in order to avoid problems. He has a withdrawn personality. His apparent activity is really agitation, and underneath, anxiety.

High initial stroke: Vanity; greed; stubbornness.

Initial arch-like stroke: Arrogance; good, expensive taste; self-indulgence.

Arched initial stroke and clubbed, vertical end-stroke: Vanity; fatuity; despotism.

Long end-stroke without a superfluous initial stroke: Materialistic pursuits beyond the capability of the writer. Irascibility; brutality; latent depression.

End-stroke launching upward:
Quick-tempered, choleric,
ambitious person.

Narrow: Inhibition; frustration;
avariciousness.

*Enlarged in the words "me" or
"myself":* Cowardly, dishonest,
unsociable, and arrogant
person.

*Wide garlanded strokes that reach
below the baseline* (check with
your magnifing glass):
Depression; neurosis.

Angular: Perseverance; will
power; harshness; selfishness.
The person is principled and
trustworthy, but not obliging.
Hard-working, ambitious
person.

Unfinished, suspended strokes:
Lying; timidity; sensitivity;
vulnerability. He is unsure of
himself.

End-stroke slightly upward:
Envious, vulnerable person.
He can be susceptible,
sensitive.

Round end-stroke: Generosity;
friendliness; good humor.

Simplified: Well-balanced and educated person.

Knotted loop on top: Perseverance; dissimulation; discretion; lying.

Simplified: Well-balanced, honest person.

Closed with a covered stroke: Good concentration; discretion; honesty.

Ringlets: Diplomacy; charm; friendliness; selfishness; cunning; hedonism; business acumen.

Coiled: Tenacity; stubbornness; inhibition; narcissism; neurosis; psychosis. Double-dealing, lying person.

Variety of shapes of the same letter: Mental instability; hypocrisy; dishonesty. The writer is untrustworthy and unprincipled. Neurosis; psychosis.

Clockwise stroke: Greedy, materialistic, and cunning, dishonest person.

Open below: The person lies, steals, cheats, swindles, and will yield to any temptation.

Open on top: Sociability, friendliness. The writer is talkative, undiplomatic, and can be slanderous.

Wide or large: Feminine; sensible, and affectionate person who loves food and other pleasures. Hedonism.

Larger than surrounding letters: Juvenile enthusiasm; immaturity; credulousness.

Smaller than surrounding letters (a characteristic especially seen in vowels): The writer has suffered from deprivation and poverty in the past. He is vindictive.

Thin: The person is mean, selfish, inhibited, materialistic, neurotic, and hoards money.

Heart-shaped: Anxiety; cardiovascular problems; anguish.

Simplified: Well-balanced and educated person.

Convex: Imagination, creativity, conceit, vanity, arrogance.

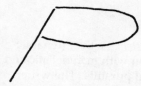

Wide: "Feminine" qualities; generosity; ambivalence.

Coiled or embellished: Business acumen; lack of intelligence and education; selfishness; conceit.

Disconnected: Neurosis.

Simplified: Well-balanced and educated person.

Knotted loop: Perseverance.

Coiled: Business acumen; selfishness.

Angular: Dynamic, ambitious, callous, materialistic, principled, and trustworthy person.

Round end-stroke: Friendliness; generosity; indolence. Weak, easily influenced person.

Long stem: Active, dynamic person with materialistic and sexual pursuits. The writer needs to be very active physically, and to practice sports.

Stem extends into baseline below, making it difficult to read: Disorder; confused mind; lack of education and principles. The person can lie, steal, and yield to forbidden temptation. He needs physical activity.

Stem that extends high up and far down: Unrealistic ambitions; lethargy; hypocrisy; lying; frustration.

Overlapping strokes: Anxiety; hypocrisy; lying; dissimulation.

Hooks on stem: Greed; dishonesty; selfishness.

Clubbed vertical stem: Deviated emotions; sexual fantasies; frustration; alcohol or drug abuse; latent neurosis.

Short or thin stem: Sexual ambivalence; weak libido; platonic, idealistic concept of sex; lethargy; timidity.

Stems of different lengths in words with double "p": Faithless in intimate relationships; the writer has numerous sexual partners.

Simplified: Well-balanced and educated person.

Coiled or embellished: Vanity; lack of intelligence.

Simplified: Well-balanced person.

Horizontal stroke on the bottom: Repressed aggression and sexuality; inhibitions; neurosis; inner conflicts.

Long stem: Dynamic person with a strong libido.

Long, clubbed stem: Sexual frustration; alcohol or drug abuse; sometimes indicates excessive smoking.

Thin, weak, or tapered stem: Regressive weakened libido; laziness; precarious health.

Short or barely visible stem: Repression; inhibitions; weak libido.

Long initial stroke: Critical mind; the writer is cautious.

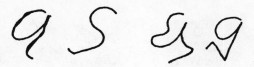

Twisted: Mental or physical suffering; sexual ambivalence; homosexuality; thyroid problems.

Simplified: Well-balanced person.

Embelished: Vanity; lying; dishonesty; stupidity.

Simplified: Well-balanced and educated person with an unusually quick, sharp, and analytical mind.

Capital used as lower-case letter: Creativity; imagination. If these capital letters appear too often, however, the person is psychotic.

Simplified: Honest, well-educated person.

Coiled: Business acumen; greed; hypocrisy; avariciousness.

Simplified, script-like: Well-balanced, educated, and intelligent person.

Closed letter with knotted loops: Perseverance; materialism; greed; selfishness. The person is possessive and can be jealous. Business acumen; lying; dissimulation; avariciousness.

High stem with knotted loop: Vanity; sensitivity; vulnerability. The person is ambitious, selfish, possessive, easily tempted, and may steal.

Stroke dropping below the baseline: The person is tired and depressed, without the strength to fulfill his aims.

End-stroke extending to the left in connected script: The person is intelligent and cunning, and can prove arrogant and may lie.

Unfinished, suspended stroke: Timidity; dishonesty; vulnerability; lying.

Simplified: Well-balanced and educated person.

Concave: Sense of humor.

Convex: Imagination; dreams; authoritarian personality.

Embellished: Stupidity; vanity.

Simplified with equal pressure and a short strong horizontal stroke in the upper zone: Well-balanced, ambitious, dynamic person with strong will power and energy.

Knotted loop: Perseverance and will power.

Undulating horizontal stroke: Sense of humor; happy disposition.

Clubbed horizontal stroke: Authority; inner tension; sexual ambivalence.

Horizontal downward stroke: Despotism.

Short upward end-stroke instead of a horizontal crossing: Sensitive, vulnerable personality.

Long launching upward stroke: Juvenile enthusiasm; quick temper; anger, irascibility; energy; vitality.

Short, weak stroke placed to the left of the stem: Lack of will power and ambition. The person lives in the past.

Horizontal stroke placed to the right of the stem: Optimism; ambition; will power; open and quick mind. Sometimes indicates carelessness.

Clubbed horizontal stroke, short and placed low: Humility; solitude; depression; career frustration.

Weak, barely noticeable horizontal stroke: The writer is timid, easily influenced, friendly, helpful, weak, indolent. He is indecisive, with a weak libido.

Long and tapering horizontal stroke: The writer's ambitions are greater than his ability to achieve them. Frustrated, he can become dishonest and even criminal (if confirmed by other signs in his writing).

Short, tapered horizontal stroke:
Caustic humor; sarcasm;
destructive tendencies.

Convex stroke over the stem: The
person is despotic and
unwilling to accommodate
others' wishes.

*Disconnected convex stroke high
above the stem:* Imagination;
dreams; mysticism; visions;
utopianism.

Backward, angular strokes: The
person is vengeful, envious,
nasty, spiteful, and aggressive.

No horizontal stroke: Laziness; no
will power or energy. However,
if the slant is extremely
progressive, the person is
passionately involved with his
work and shows great will
power.

*Variety of different shapes of the
same letter:* Instability;
carelessness; fluctuating will
power and humor. Neurosis;
deceit. The person is
untrustworthy and can lie.

Simplified: Well-balanced and educated person.

Angular, similar to the letter "V": Ambition; tenacity; aggression; virility. The person can be nasty, but he is reliable.

Simplified: Well-balanced and educated person.

Thread-like: Diplomatic, quick-minded, irritable, unstable, distant, and nervous person.

Large: Generosity; friendliness, affection; sensuality; hedonism.

Large, falling underneath the baseline: Depression.

Angular: Will power; principles; honesty; harshness; unwillingness to accommodate others' wishes. The person cannot be influenced, is not affectionate, and can be nasty. Hard-working, ambitious character.

Disconnected: Anguish; split personality; dishonesty; schizophrenia; lying.

Long initial stroke: The writer is careful, with a critical and analytical mind.

High launching upward end-stroke: Irascible, the person has fits of irrepressible anger; choleric temper.

Simplified: Well-educated.

Embellished: Low intelligence; greed; lying; hypocrisy.

Launching upward end-stroke: Quick, explosive temper; juvenile enthusiasm.

Simplified: Well-balanced and educated person.

Thread-like: Diplomacy; instability. The person is irritable and nervous, and can dissimulate and lie.

Backward end-stroke: Greed; inhibitions; anxiety; lying.

Garlanded: Friendliness; femininity; weakness. The writer is affectionate and easily influenced.

Disconnected strokes that alter the letter: Split personality.

Embellished with superfluous knotted loops: Business acumen; lying; materialism; selfishness; stubbornness.

Strange, "pornographic" looking shapes: Fantasies of debauchery; sexual ambivalence.

Launching upward end-stroke: Quick-temper; anger; unwillingness to accommodate others' wishes; and diplomacy.

Simplified: Well-balanced person.

Long descendant stroke: The writer is materialistic, aggressive, vengeful, and may have depressive tendencies.

Disconnected: The person has a split personality and can be slanderous.

Simplified: Well-balanced person.

Strokes below the baseline: Impatient and angry person.

Disconnected: Neurosis.

Simplified: Well-balanced.

Round backward stem: The person is easily influenced. Sexual ambivalence.

Simplified: Well-balanced.

Coils or hooks: Greed; selfishness; dishonesty; lying.

Weak tapered stem: Weak libido.

Short stem: Weak libido; asceticism.

Large or open backward loop: Sexual ambivalence. Tapered end-stroke indicates destructive tendencies.

Simplified script-like: Well-balanced, educated, dynamic, and ambitious person.

Soft curves similar to the letter "S": Friendliness; diplomacy; affectionate nature.

Simplified: Well-balanced and educated person.

Launching upward end-stroke: Brutality; anger; quick-temper.

Clubbed, horizontal end-stroke: Sexual problems and ambivalence. The person pushes his friends away with unexpected brutality.

Tapered end-stroke: Destructive tendencies.

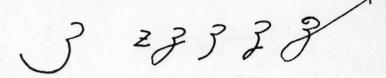

Open backward loop:
Homosexuality. The person
dissimulates and lies.

Variety of shapes of the same letter:
Instability; neurosis; lying.

Put down on paper whatever you discovered in the samples you
are analyzing through your study of the alphabet.

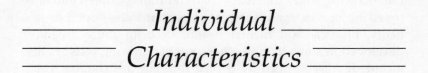

2
Individual
Characteristics

Through study of the first chapter you have acquired the basic knowledge necessary to analyze handwriting. To recognize the principal character traits through handwriting, train yourself to compare samples. If two hands are never identical, they can nevertheless be very similar, in which case the meaning of the dominant character trait will be the same. The traits discovered through this method will be more pronounced in the person analyzed than in most others.

In this chapter the teaching method is reversed: the traits are outlined, accompanied by the handwriting signs that define them. This will help you to broaden and apply what you have studied thus far. There are certain characteristics you hope to find in your friends or business partners that you imagine to be most compatible with your own psychological and perhaps physical make-up. For example, one man might look for a friendly, amusing, and affectionate woman friend; he does not mind if she lies or dates other men. On the contrary, another man may want a faithful and honest woman even if she is dull and unimaginative. Suppose you need a trustworthy business partner; if a prospective partner is a stranger, a study of his handwriting will tell you all about him. (A professional thief, for example, can use handwriting analysis to find someone who can steal without suffering from a bad conscience.) You will find in the following pages the major character traits outlined and illustrated by one or more samples. Important areas such as sexuality, physical and mental health, or drug abuse are more developed in some than in others; simple drawing tests are also included. All you need do is read through this chapter. Later, when you try to analyze your friends' handwriting in search of a particular trait, you can refer to the appropriate page and study the sample illustrating the quality you seek; if it shows some similarity, you can be certain that that trait applies to your subject.

All the samples in this chapter are new. Their study will help you expand your experience.

PERSONALITY TRAITS

Accuracy.

doesn't really bother me too just prevents me from taking outside and enjoying the colours of autumn. Perhaps that is

Normal margins, spacing, and size; straight or slightly meandering baseline; regular pressure; letters simplified in shape.

Adaptability.

time and place.

I hope this

sufficient for your

Letters of round or garlanded shape; no angular strokes or hooks.

Affectivity.

days the newspapers

still as sweet as

Round, connected writing of medium or strong pressure spread out mainly in the middle zone. The size of the letters is medium to large; the spacing between words and lines is not too large. Garlanded strokes are possible.

Aggression.

Peter's little sister

polyglot abilities.

Angular; progressive slant (not always); long, tapering end-strokes launching upward.

Ambition.

finish here.

anytime soon

Fast and progressive script; ascendant baseline; angular, or a mixture of angular and round strokes in the letters.

Amiability.

or tea together

Garlanded or round script; no angles, hooks, or arcades.

Analytical-mindedness.

her degree.
the moment and could not come

Pau's —

Connected script; sometimes the dot of the "i" is connected to the following letter; straight or slightly meandering baseline.

Anger.

Angular strokes; end-strokes launch upward.

Arrogance.

Arcades in small or capital letters or in connecting strokes.

Asceticism.

Today I reflected upon

assistant

Sparse lower and middle zone; the script extends mainly towards the upper zone. Some strokes can be too high. Light pressure.

Authoritativeness.

but

necessitates

been leaking - Rugs I've tried to patch

Convex horizontal stroke of the letter "t"; stick-like strokes reaching below the lower zone. Speedy writing; some tapered end-strokes.

Caution.

still nice, is snow in the mountains now.

Collaboration

Long initial stroke; sometimes a dot appears after the signature or at the end of the envelope address.

Conscientiousness.

letter, but I really do want nonsense about you being attractive with absolutely

Readable, well-spaced script on a straight or slightly meandering baseline; regular, average pressure.

Creativity.

manual creativity

Since my vet ocean, I have locate only one

Heavy pressure; slow writing with one or two capital letters in the middle of a word; spread out in the middle and lower zone; rather large script without any particular slant.

Shakespeare & Co

intellectual creativity

> in New York
> art & literature
> than Bennington
> will amount to some

Simplified, speedy writing; light pressure; progressive slant.

Cruelty.

> whiff also does that
> the covers from
> I saw three

Angular or tapering strokes; hooks; heavy pressure; little space between letters; launching upward or long stick-like strokes.

Decisiveness.

I am glad that you are able

Speedy and simplified writing; progressive slant; straight baseline; regular pressure.

Diplomacy.

two moves

in English

I have to admit

Meandering baseline; speedy, progressive, and sometimes altered writing. Coils, hooks, and covered strokes can appear as well as garlands and threads.

Economy.

ders here an so
so abundant
thing to do is
things 5-80 8

5. Every man has within himself
these four virtues: Humanity, right-
eousness, decorum and wisdom. The
man who considers himself incapable
of exercising them is destroying himself

Dear Diane
I came back by 8:00pm
but have to get back to

Small or tight script; some covered strokes; straight baseline.
The slant can be regressive, but not necessarily.

Egotism.

Martin,
Far from
geographically & otherwis'
but the people here are
great + the scenery

Tight, confusing, altered, and reversed script; tight spacing;
size can be large, small or medium.

Energy.

visit me on 9th Street. I
have found a great restaurant
on Broadway, where tea
and scones are very cheap

Speedy writing on a straight or slightly meandering baseline; the pressure is regular, usually medium or strong. The letter "t" shows a short, strong, and regular horizontal stroke. The slant is vertical or progressive; in extremely progressive script the "t" stroke is of less importance.

Fidelity.

Dear Claude,

My first impulse
you in my arms and

The baseline is rather straight and most letters reaching the lower zone are the same shape and length.

Flexibility.

still writing Hollywood &
He makes a lot of money but
it the fact that not much of

Speedy, round or garlanded writing on a meandering baseline; size small or medium; no coils or angles; sometimes ringlets.

Friendliness.

not too far from her.

Round or garlanded shapes; ringlets.

Generosity.

It has been a long track. I got ill — to the states again. Here is my

Round or garlanded shapes; long, slightly concave end-strokes; large letters; connections spread out in the middle zone; generous spacing between words.

Gentleness.

continue to study it have one brother who a passion for cats

Weak pressure; round or garlanded shapes; rather small size; middle zone predominant; upper and lower zones almost disappear.

Greed.

... ing I would never have come here
... celebrate my first Bastille Day,
... ops engaging board of directors,
Whitman, the charming Sylva,
d Bashorville, whose unflappa —
ll, & who put us to shame by being
r enough to wear a tie on the
main here a long time .

Tight spacing; entangled letters with coils and hooks; reversed
or tapering strokes; strong pressure; embellished script.

Harshness (Callousness).

very interesting
view of the project.
Write me a letter
you have been keeping

Greetings. How are the
How was George's trip? h
but exciting for me at the
I'm in production on two

INformation oN (handwritten)

Angular strokes, sometimes in the lower loops; tapering end-strokes; twisted, covered letters; medium to strong pressure; coiled, stick-like, and clubbed strokes often appearing at the end of a word and extending beyond the lower zone; straight baseline; reversed angles; generous spacing.

Humility.

Newspaper a (handwritten)
The thing I'm most (handwritten)
read. I have been stu (handwritten)
ife, and will probably (handwritten)

Light pressure; small size; short capital letters with a slight backward slant; unfinished strokes.

Humor.

will be (handwritten)

Concave initial stroke; meandering, horizontal "t" crossing; straight or progressive slant.

Hypocrisy.

CALL After 3 Pm   I
WRITE my Father
Paying the Teleph
You Wouldn't write

Reversed slant; covered strokes; unfinished letters.

Idealism.

attended classes

High stems reaching above the upper zone.

Imagination.

interested in

Very high dots on the letter "i."

Immaturity.

I am very
working for your famous
took an English

experience

Slow, very regular, and schoolish writing.

Impatience.

to go back to school seem
I have a few friends who
careers after extra schooling.
regret they didn't do it Earlier -

Speedy writing; light pressure; unfinished strokes; thread-like words.

Infidelity.

Paris et je
sa, il ne fait pas très
moment - J'spère que
Je n'affrête à aller

A great variety of stems and loops in the lower zone.

Inhibition.

It was seven o'clock.

much for dinner on Tuesday
the cheese! I pound the

Backward slant; tight letters, sometimes in a forward or straight slant; unfinished strokes and words.

Instability.

'e couch even to go a the
& anything done, and I
nize, which I generally

Light pressure; meandering baseline.

Intelligence.

Dear George,
Remember me? That Chinese American fellow
from the Seattle/Portland area who used to
hang out at your place for what seemed like
years? I found this post card and it so.

(Quick understanding of a situation and the ability to find good solutions to problems.)

Speedy writing; regular, usually light pressure; small size; progressive slant; few coils and hooks; mixed round and angular strokes; connected letters mixed with some juxtaposed letters within words.

Intuition.

Company on board

August. All our best

Disconnected script.

Jealousy.

to an occasional commer
mostly doing NABET pi
Bought a small builden
in Brooklyn last fall
and when I'm not on a

Knotted loops in the letters "s"; straight baseline; very progressive slant.

Joy in living.

that the results analysis don't reveal ange or weird secrets

Progressive slant; slightly ascendant baseline; strong or medium pressure.

Laziness.

*, the water suddenly gushed
ubilation I pulled the tap out
water spurt everywhere with
sible to push the tap back in.
perservered for fifteen minutes
the flood. Water continued to
into the bedroom.
the day.*

Slow writing; round shapes; reversed strokes; open backward loops in the lower zone.

Libido.

In graphology, libido means joy in living, will power, and sexuality (*See also* these words.)

Low intelligence (adult over 25 years old).

Very slow and embellished script; reversed slant; jumbled, confused handwriting.

Loyalty.

Straight or slightly meandering baseline; progressive or upward slant; regular size; regular pressure; very few signs that indicate lying (see entry for "lying").

Lying.

A person can tell minor lies out of politeness in daily life without showing any signs of lying in his handwriting. When these signs appear and are numerous (let's say four or five), then you can be sure that the writer lies more than the average person. It is important to detect these signs: a business partner or an intimate friend who lies all the time is a serious disability.

There are twenty-six signs that indicate lying. Individually they do not necessarily have this meaning. Suppose you have the first six signs in your handwriting and venture to wipe them out; this is possible, but you will probably develop some of the other twenty signs in your script. To change one's handwriting completely is just as difficult as painting a "false" Rembrandt and selling it as a real one.

You should often refer to this section to properly acquaint yourself with these important signs.

1. jumbled, and impossible-to-read script

2. meandering baseline with light pressure

3. coiled letters

4. changing slant

5. reversed slant or strokes

6. slow, contrived script

7. altered letters

8. jumbled (but legible) lines

9. unfinished strokes or letters

10. thread-like script

11. arcades in letters or connecting strokes

12. covered strokes

13. flourished letters

14. tapered strokes or words

15. varying sizes of letters

16. improved or corrected strokes in already written words

17. hooks

18. several very different handwritings by the same person

19. capital letters reaching below the baseline

20. end-strokes of "n" or "m" plunging into the lower zone

21. superfluous or heavy dots in the script or at the end of the envelope address

22. very different handwritings in signature and envelope address

23. odd, irregular spacing and pressure

24. irregular speed of writing

25. "a" and "o" open at the bottom or written with clockwise strokes

26. oversized letter "I"

Samples belonging to liars:

Six signs: Embellished, reversed, coiled, and hooked strokes, in a slow, artificial writing.

Seven signs: Varying sizes of letters; tapering strokes; coils; strange, irregular spacing; arcades; reversed angles.

Six signs: Light pressure; meandering baseline; heavy dots on the "i"; hooks; reversed open loops and strokes in the lower zone; unfinished letters; tapered end-strokes.

Handwritten sample:

> Thursday 24
> Do hope they are right to
> translate "representer"
> as "almshouse". We walked
> through just such a little
> hospie yesterday, with all
> the roses in full bloom, and

Ten signs (Such a high number indicates mental illness—myth-omania): Light pressure; changing, reversed slant; meandering baseline; coils; hooks; altered letters; tapered strokes; uneven spacing; jumbled lines; covered strokes.

Handwritten sample:

> We were asked by Mr Anthony Dunn
> of Lee, Bolton & Lee to introduce
> ourselves. Sue, my wife was Mr

Ten signs: Light, irregular pressure; clubbed strokes; changing speed; covered strokes; reversed angles; altered letters; suspended and tapered end-strokes; coils; meandering baseline.

Handwritten sample:

> gorgeous. Hopefully, I'll
> come out of my dry spell
> soon. Thanks for watching
> for my mail. I've found
> out there are some very import

Five signs: Jumbled lines; covered strokes; coils; reversed strokes; altered letters.

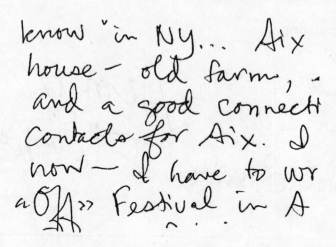

Seven signs: Light pressure; meandering baseline; tapered end-strokes; reversed angles; overlapping strokes; hooks (use your magnifying glass); changing slant.

Six signs: Light pressure; thread-like script; altered letters that are impossible to read; reversed end-strokes; odd, irregular spacing.

NOTE: All these signs are very precise; they are the result of personal research during many years of applied graphology. When you count more than four or five, you can be certain that the person you are analyzing lies almost constantly. The subject will, of course, try to protest, but will be stunned by your discovery.

Manipulation.

badly as
been better

George
Stakes

Krudaare Simsby

Arcades.

Materialism

for

yhe

Dear Mr. Whitman,
I came here after about a
decade of expectation,
expecting to find the
world's best bookstore.

Script mainly in the middle zone; long, stick-like, slightly clubbed stems reaching below the lower zone; tight spacing; loops; coils; strong pressure.

Meanness.

Shakespeare Company

Dearest all :
After treking through the Pyrenne
down through Granada (the Alhan
and to Gibralter, with Amanda. Tob

them 'everywhere. I even
his house, and touched —

Tight spacing; reversed angles; narrow margins; small size; tapered strokes; sometimes disconnected, progressive script; coils and hooks.

Moodiness.

forget to do anyon
don't. Anyway,
the food this morning
The very fout that
at that time

Very meandering baseline; various slants and sizes; reversed angular strokes; several completely different handwritings; varying pressure.

Optimism.

hor of poems and the
And where else can
be at home with his

Speedy writing; progressive slant; slightly ascending baseline.

Parsimony.

was returned

Without her prompt
'e so wonderfully i
I have met the s

stayed there for only one day
we didn't like the city. The
too much crime there. But a
we hope. you like to get a

4. Don't take anything for granted, upon the bare authority of an author; but weigh and consider in your own mind, the probability of the facts (Guru, Feb, 1986)

Abrupt end-strokes; tight spacing; small size; narrow margins.

Passion.

wonderful duck cooked in sauce. It seems that lack of home it the meal is than I remember it.

because you

Very progressive slant; straight baseline; no right margin.

Perseverance.

let a few

Knotted loops.

Pessimism.

Dear Claude, I've just discovered that I must work late on Wed. night, so I'm sorry I won't make " happy to help

Descendant baselines and end-strokes; letters reaching below their normal zone; descendant signature placed towards the left side; very small capital letters; very generous spacing.

Possessiveness.

of July. 'Tried to avoid crowds. 'Been working in the last year and a course

Knotted loops in the letter "s."

Punctuality.

should often refer back to th
with the following signs
    personal research

Straight baseline; regular spacing.

Rectitude.

l pleasure meeting
Book fair in Frankfurt
your books on

Straight baseline; regular size, slant, and pressure.

Reliability.

By the way. I'm
you reassured me
masculinity - espe

Straight or slightly meandering baseline; vertical or progressive, regular slant, regular size and shape; regular pressure; few signs that indicate lying.

Romanticism

Since ⌐ these events, I have
three years, which in it
but except for a number c
self inflicted, life has generall
Paris now⁺ with the intentic
can only hope that a til
reading "Is Paris Drowning?" 1

Light pressure; round shapes; concave end-strokes; slightly regressive slant.

Selfishness.

having me for dinner + tea
My best to you and your
commune — I hope to cross
pathe again someday

rupped to pick up
different topics
plf madce thy nl

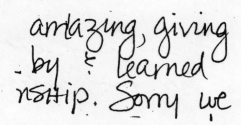

No margins; very large or tight spacing; abrupt end-strokes; stick-like strokes plunging downward; reversed slant (not always); very small size or large size; tapered strokes.

Sensitivity.

Light pressure; unfinished strokes and end-strokes; thread-like script.

Shyness.

Light pressure; unfinished letters and strokes; small size; reversed slant.

Spontaneity.

To me and let you are and where

Speedy writing; progressive slant; clear and easy-to-read script.

Stubbornness.

I was born in.
My Parents are
accommodation
meets with

Here's hoping you get
I got to spend time

Slow writing; backward slant; monotonous aspect; coils.

Thievery.

discordont kept
of ducks. langage

school, we moved to
in a two-storey house.

Coils and hooks; reversed angular strokes; "a" and "o" open at the bottom.

Trustworthiness.

of me, how is
you? Are you
busy as always
away, typing

Straight baseline; regular shapes and sizes; regular pressure; few signs that indicate lying; no backward strokes or slant.

Unreliability.

you are for once

a good conversation

one will be meeting

Very meandering baseline; light pressure; retouched strokes; numerous signs that indicate lying.

Vengefulness (Spitefulness).

weekend we can go
enjoy ourselves without
thought either one of us
be studying.
The first weekend

Reversed, angular, and tapered strokes.

Virility.

eyed beautiful baby

Minneapolis

Speedy, small writing; closed loops; importance of middle and lower zone; sometimes angular, stick-like strokes.

Vitality.

We will be here

Speedy writing; progressive slant; strong and regular pressure.

Vulnerability.

I enjoy watching among themselves on they laugh, they sing. more than we know

Unfinished strokes; tapered; slightly launching upward end-strokes.

Will power.

has just return

Short and strong horizontal "t" crossings.

Wit.

ever seen a more amaz-
, if I had to leave

Speedy and small writing.

PHYSICAL HEALTH

Good health.

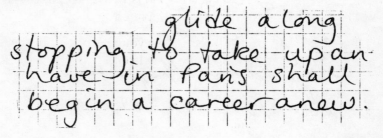

glide along
stopping to take up an
have in Paris shall
begin a career anew.

Clear, regular handwriting with strong pressure. The letters are never twisted or broken.

Here follows an outline of particular health problems, and the signs that reveal them.

Alzheimer's disease.

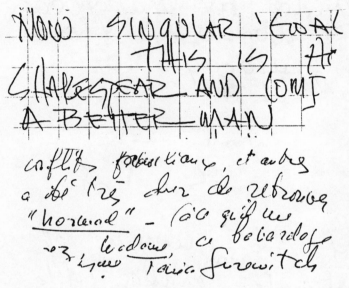

The general condition of the person is weakened; his nervous system and his brain function are impaired.

Symptoms of senility can occur in a younger person following alcohol or drug abuse, as will be seen later.

Asthma.

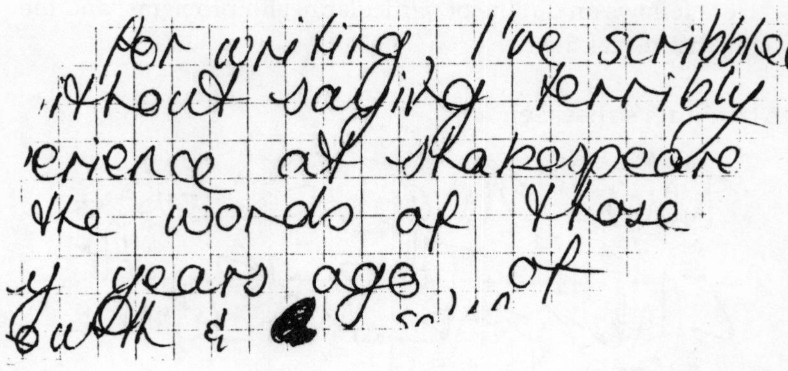

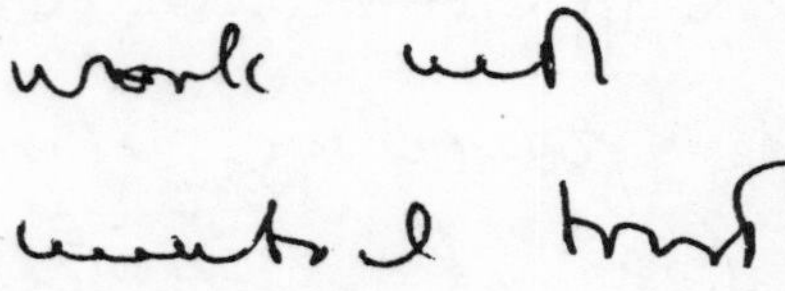

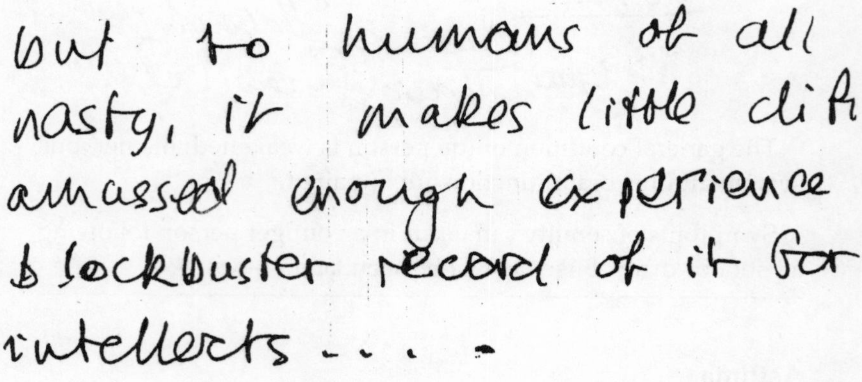

[handwritten sample:]

for writing, I've scribbled
without saying terribly
erience at Shakespeare
the words of those
y years ago, of
earth & so on

work with

until I trust

but to humans of all
nasty, it makes little diff
amassed enough experience
blockbuster record of it for
intellects ... -

This ailment is sometimes psychosomatic. The person has difficulty breathing and controlling his emotions; he is anguished and often afraid of choking.

The handwriting shows: irregularities (intense emotions); imprecise and useless improvements (anguish); various, often descendant end-strokes (anxiety) inflated upper loops that can be reversed (shortness of breath); broken strokes (breathing problems); very generous spacing in a monotonous script (deviated and blocked affections); superfluous dots (respiratory problems).

All of these signs are not necessarily present. Other meanings are possible, such as depression and neurosis.

NOTE: It is not possible to detect asthma with 100 percent accuracy. We can only suspect that the writer suffers from it.

Bronchitis, tuberculosis, and other respiratory disorders.

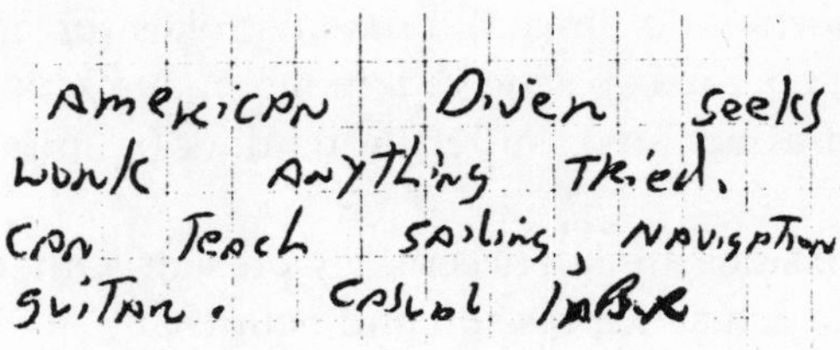

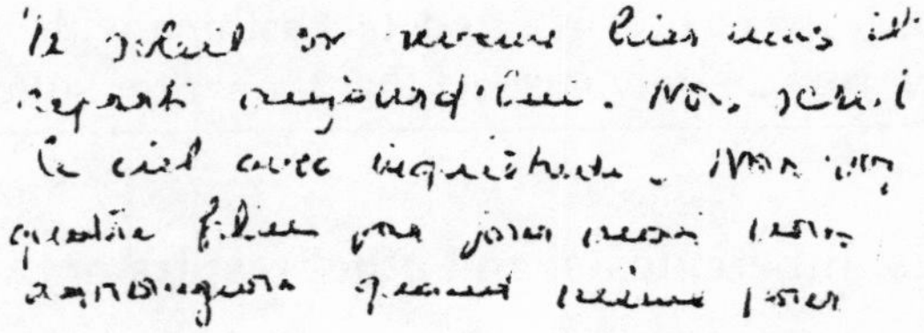

American Diver seeks work. Anything Tried. Can Teach sailing, navigation, guitar. Cabbal Intrex

[handwritten text]

The handwriting shows: Superfluous dots (the writer stops, struggles for air); weak and irregular pressure (fatigue); large spaces between lines (struggle for air); twisted or broken vertical strokes (suffering, breathing problems); letters or upper strokes missing (shortness of breath); altered letters (anguish, anxiety); round and pasty writing (weakness); horizontal stroke of "t" missing (resignation); loops in the lower zone made with heavy or irregular pressure (unsatisfactory libido); slow writing in the morning and speedy writing in the evening, including altered letters (fever).

All of these signs are not necessarily present in any given subject's handwriting.

Cancer.

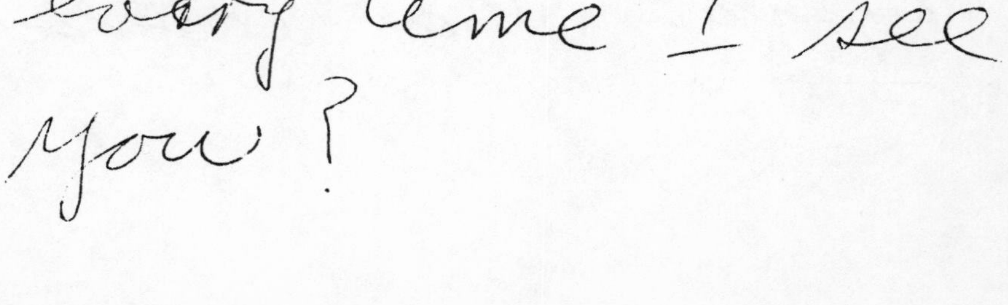

every time I see you?

[handwriting sample]

[handwriting sample]

[handwriting sample: Olympiad in Nice. The brought a tremendous selling well but left unsold at]

This disease cannot be detected in its early stages. Towards the end of the illness, when the person becomes generally weak, these traits begin to show in the handwriting: altered letters (poor concentration); twisted and broken strokes (suffering, irregular heart beat); very weak and irregular pressure (fatigue); descendant baselines and end-strokes (depression); larger or smaller writing; trembling strokes.

Cardiovascular disorders.

high blood pressure

Poul,

thanks a lot.

Madame

salutations   *Parfumerie.*

Thin or broken strokes in stems or loops.

NOTE: This sign is precise and relatively easy to detect.

---

other heart disorders

us by the barbarous old
Dear!, for making
a beer!

prestations

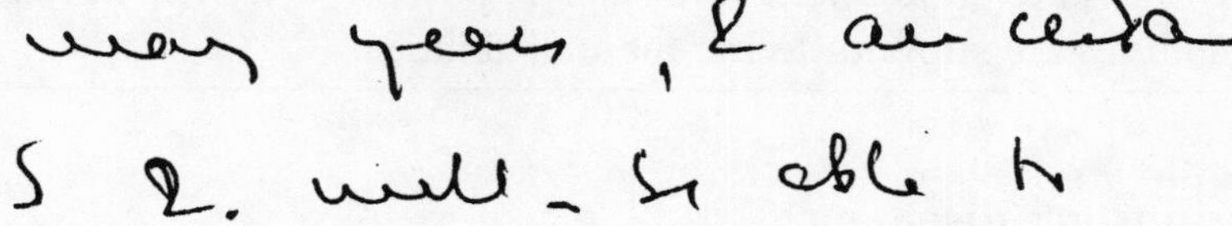

[handwritten sample]

Pasty, filled with ink.

Numerous physical ailments.

Sample of a seventy-two-year-old woman:

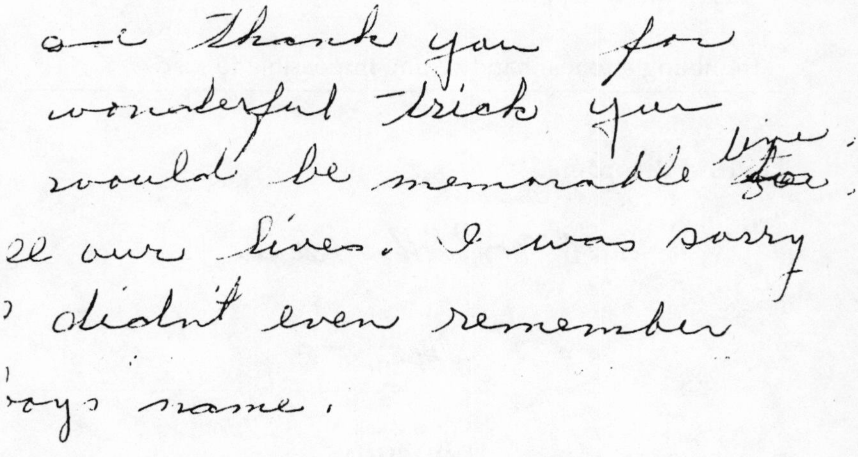

[handwritten sample]

Light pressure; twisted letters; meandering baseline; light and irregular "t" crossings; connected script; easy-to-read handwriting; launching upward end-strokes.

PORTRAIT: The subject is in good mental health in spite of her numerous physical ailments (twisted strokes). She is a sociable and generous woman who still has some juvenile enthusiasm. At times she explodes into an outburst of anger, and there are some tendencies towards inner instability. Joy in living and spontaneity are also apparent. Her intellectual abilities are superior to her manual abilities.

Parkinson's disease.

Trembling strokes; handwriting impossible to read.

Thyroid disorders.

These problems usually appear during adolescence, and if they persist can cause numerous complications. Twisted strokes or reversed loops in the middle and lower zones often occur.

Ulcers.

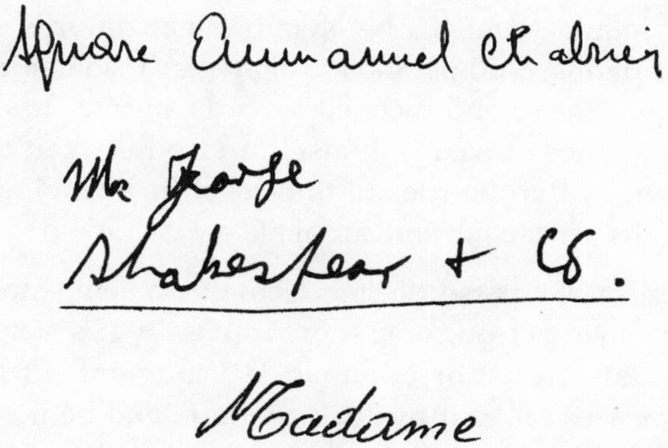

[handwriting sample: "Square Annamuel Chalney"]

[handwriting sample: "Mr George"]

[handwriting sample: "Shakespear + Co."]

[handwriting sample: "Madame"]

Like asthma, ulcers can be provoked through psychic or emotional processes. Twisted strokes in the middle and upper zones (suffering) and heavy pressure (struggle against the ailment) often occur.

MENTAL HEALTH

It is easier to ascertain the mental health of a person than to pinpoint his various physical ailments. However, anyone who has studied psychoanalysis must agree that the lines between neurosis, psychosis, and schizophrenia are not always easy to draw. To simplify matters the following characterizations may be applied:

1. A _neurotic_ person suffers from repeated periods of depression, cyclic moods, unstable emotions, mania and paranoia,

and sexual dysfunction; these problems make his private life difficult for himself and for those living with him.

2. The *psychotic* person finds it difficult to distinguish reality from an imaginary state of being. Sometimes he feels guilty about acts he commits only in his imagination, whereas certain acts that have really occurred do not bother him at all. He can be sadomasochistic; he is ambivalent towards sex. His anxiety, phobia, and paranoia will intensify; sometimes he is manic-depressive and inclined towards suicide. His general destructiveness towards himself and others can be overwhelming. Often he tries to find relief in alcohol and drug abuse. His private life and social life are disturbed.

3. The *schizophrenic* person suffers from the same phenomena as the psychotic person, only more intensely. His state can be stable, dangerous, or criminal. His moments of lucidity, when he sees life as it really is, are rare, and he is confused most of the time. In his unaware state, he can be quite happy. His libido does not function normally. His *private life, social life,* and *professional life* fall apart. Many violent criminals and drug addicts are schizophrenic.

Like fever in physical diseases, certain symptoms will repeat themselves throughout these three groups, and will simply be more or less intense according to the seriousness of the person's mental state. Once you have analyzed a number of samples belonging to people suffering from poor mental health, it will be easy for you to detect such disorders. Do not forget that people with mental health disorders can be highly intelligent and well-educated but are never easy to live or work with. Therefore it is extremely useful to be able to determine someone's mental health through the study of his handwriting when you are looking for the "ideal" romantic or business partner.

Also, a person's mental health invariably influences his physical health. Mental health disorders are partly endogenous and partly environmental. They often recur in families and are very difficult to cure. It is useless to tell the victim of such a disorder to stop being depressed, agitated, or drug-addicted. He is unable to do so, although psychoanalysis and certain medications prescribed by psychiatrists can stabilize his condition and permit him to resume his social and professional life, to a certain extent.

We will study in detail samples of neurotics, psychotics, and schizophrenics. You will soon see the differences and the similarities among them.

Substance abusers are also analyzed in the following section.

Neurosis.

reactional neurosis

The writer is depressed for a specific reason. Perhaps he has lost a beloved family member or a dear friend; perhaps his profession is unsatisfying; he may have lost his job. His depression will only be temporary, unlikely to exceed a few weeks or months. Usually the change that occurs is a descendant baseline. Certain letters and end-strokes will also extend below their normal zone. As soon as the writer feels better, the baseline will return to horizontal. This sign is the same whether the writer is an adult or a child. The sample on the previous page belongs to a homesick girl of eleven who is otherwise well-balanced.

---

chronic neurosis

This is a genuine mental health disorder because it reappears regularly without any particular external cause. Three main reasons for chronic neurosis are:

physical predisposition

environment

trauma at an early age, or when in a weakened condition.

Often all three factors are present, making the condition more difficult to reverse. Years of psychoanalysis, chemical therapy, and, in some cases, *graphotherapy* are needed to lessen the mental sufferings of the person.

Symptoms of chronic neurosis:

1. sudden depression

2. extreme feelings of guilt for crimes not committed

3. muteness

4. mythomania—attempting to flee reality

5. general instability (continually changing friends, professions, and residences), cyclic moods

6. great suffering, anguish, and anxiety for no discernible reason.

7. weakened libido

8. self-centeredness

9. irresponsibility

Ways to detect these symptoms in handwriting:

1. *Depression:* Baseline is slightly descendant; some letters plunge below the baseline. Capital letters show a backward slant in a generally progressive or straight handwriting.

2. *Excessive, misplaced guilt:* Reversed strokes; weak pressure; unfinished and broken letters and tapering words. The signature is on the left side, below the message.

3. *Muteness:* Very large margins all around the written message; altered letters that are difficult to read. Generous spacing between words and lines.

4. *Mythomania:* Detected by eight or more signs that reveal lying (*see* "lying.")

5. *Instability:* Extremely meandering baseline; various slants; weak pressure.

6. *Anguish, anxiety:* Altered, retouched strokes. (The writer often goes back to already written words and tries to improve their appearance.)

7. *Weakened libido:* Vertical tapered stems that hang limply and without loops below the baseline. Sometimes the lower zone is barely visible. Weak pressure.

8. *Self-centeredness:* No end-strokes extending to the next word. The writing may be tight and angular.

All of the above symptoms and signs do not have to be present in order to detect the illness. Here follow samples from chronically neurotic subjects. Most are analyzed in detail.

This handwriting belongs to a Russian-language student. The writer is highly intelligent but suffers from chronic depression. As he is still very young, there is hope that his instability may later disappear.

This sample shows: Speedy writing (quick mind, intelligence, impatience, good education); light pressure and meandering baseline (instability); altered, difficult to read strokes (attempts to flee reality, anxiety); varying slants (chronic instability); letters reaching below the baseline (depression); sparse lower zone (weakened libido).

This sample belongs to a woman of twenty-six, a former student of literature, who is married with two children. She is very unhappy, constantly worrying, and her marriage is a failure.

To experience . It is not . but I've been asked to , comments so I will. It's Paris and I'm worring abou enough warm clothes, Lot of

Her handwriting shows: variable pressure (instability, anxiety); meandering baseline (instability); twisted, unfinished letters (dissimulation, suffering); high upper zone (unreachable goals); generous spacing (independence, isolation, loneliness); descendant baseline (depression); lower loops narrow and long (sexual and materialistic frustration); regressive coils and strokes (selfishness, envy).

The following sample belongs to a rather hysterical woman of forty-five. She is self-centered and stereotypically feminine; she is a mythomaniac and lives alone. Her mental problems find some relief in her artistic creativity as a fashion designer. Generally designing, drawing, and painting are positive influences on the mental condition of a person.

Her handwriting is impossible to read. It's also too large and confused. It has a slight backward slant.

This sample belongs to an extremely unstable and often depressed woman of fifty-five who has been in psychoanalysis most of her life.

Her handwriting shows: a very meandering baseline (instability); varying slant (instability); varying pressure (deviated emotions); altered letters and strokes (anxiety); unfinished letters (dissimulation, lying); twisted and broken letters (schizophrenia, suffering); tapered strokes (use your magnifying glass) destructiveness; selfishness); irregular spacing (changeable moods, isolation); altered strokes (anxiety).

This sample belongs to a young mother of thirty-two. She is chronically depressed and has a family history of psychosis.

> Dear Claude,
> Sorry to not say goodbye
> but I hate goodbye's.
> I have found a wonderful

Her handwriting has a meandering baseline; tapered and altered strokes; irregular pressure.

NOTE: It is not necessary to explain each sample in detail. You will make more progress by seeing as many samples as possible.

The writer of the sample below is a thirty-year-old businessman. He is very nervous and suffers from chronic anxiety. He is constantly changing jobs and moving from one country to another. He is professionally and sexually frustrated.

> ld stop in @ Schakespeares
> ssaf wine at the cafe across.
> f the last time on my way through
> 're on holiday, no doubt enjoying a
> . I want to go, Do you remember your

His handwriting shows: Speedy writing (intelligence, education); varying slant (instability); meandering baseline (instability); backward strokes (attachment to the past, difficulty in overcoming problems of the past and adjusting to the present; heavy dots on the "i" (neurosis, anxiety); altered letters (anguish, doubts, distrust); tapered strokes (destructiveness, aggression); reversed angles (selfishness, vengefulness, rancor); covered strokes, coils (dissimulation, lying); abrupt end-strokes (selfishness); long initial strokes (critical mindedness, distrust); long and varying lower stems and loops (sexual frustration, infidelity); generous spacing between lines (independence, loneliness, isolation).

The sample belongs to a woman of twenty-two who wants to study languages in college. Very insecure, she is neurotically attached to her parents and friends. It is obvious that she has not chosen the right career. Her limited intelligence and intuition do not suit her studies. A manual or commercial profession would be more suitable in her case.

Her handwriting shows: Large round shapes (femininity, manual creativity, immaturity); slow writing (manual and business skills); coiled letters in the middle zone (diplomacy, dissimulation, selfishness, lying, business acumen); jumbled lines and letters, signature too close to the text (anxiety, neurotic attachment to others, confused mind); writing mainly in the lower and middle zone (materialism, need of physical exercise); connected and altered script (anxiety, paranoid tendencies, lack of intuition, immaturity); tapered strokes (aggression, destructiveness, selfishness); slightly monotonous script (immaturity; chronic neurosis); retouched letters (anxiety).

This last sample of a chronically neurotic person belongs to a man of twenty-five who works as an industrial designer. He is rather hysterical. We can analyze his personality in spite of the fact that he prints and uses capital letters.

His handwriting shows: Slow and contrived writing (slow reasoning, manual ability); meandering baseline (instability); some words plunge below the baseline (depression); tapered strokes (destructiveness, aggression); stick-like and backward strokes (virility, vengefulness, nastiness, hysteria); small hooks (greed, selfishness); monotonous script (chronic neurosis); excessively long strokes (lack of will power, anger, hysteria, callousness).

This is a case of borderline psychosis, since his problems already interfere with his social life and professional life.

Psychosis.

The signs in the handwriting and the inherent character traits of the psychotic are similar to those of the chronically neurotic, but they are more pronounced. As the writer becomes more and more removed from reality, problems arise not only in his private life but also in his social interactions and professional activity. His behavior can be odd, unpredictable, and selfish.

However, as the subject becomes increasingly indifferent towards his surroundings, his inner suffering can at times grow less acute than it was in his former state of neurosis. His condition is difficult to improve, and although he can still be influenced, his state usually deteriorates. Many psychotics become alcoholics or drug addicts in their search for relief.

In this category can be classified the psychopath, the paranoiac, the sadomasochist, the multiple personality type, the suicidal person, and the manic-depressive character. The last is a borderline case; certain psychoanalysts categorize it as schizophrenic, believing that improvement is impossible.

How do the symptoms of the psychotic show in his or her handwriting as compared to the neurotic?

1. *More instability:* Baseline is extremely meandering; varying slants, often reversed; altered letters; light pressure.

2. *Greater destructive and self-destructive tendencies:* Tapered words and strokes; reversed angles; crossed out signature (suicidal wishes).

3. *Remoteness from reality:* Speed, thread-like, difficult-to-read writing.

4. *Insecurity:* Very light pressure; unfinished letters; retouched strokes.

5. *Indifference:* Generous, irregular spacing.

6. *Schizoid state:* Odd spacing between letters or in the middle of the signature.

7. *Multiple personality:* Three, four, or more completely different handwritings in the same sample or in different samples from the same person.

8. *Deviated emotions:* Clubbed strokes.

9. *Isolation:* Very generous spacing and margins.

10. *Heightened anxiety:* Altered letters and strokes.

11. *Excessive attachment to friends:* Tight spacing and margins; confused writing.

12. *Regression:* Monotonous, slow handwriting.

13. *Weakened libido:* Short stems and loops in the lower zone.

14. *Sexual obsession:* Clubbed strokes, exaggerated lower zone, very coiled letters in the middle zone (excessive auto-erotism).

15. *Sexual ambivalence:* In a male's writing, very round or garlanded letters.

16. *Psychosis:* Heavy dots on the "i."

NOTE: A mentally disturbed person's sexuality is never normal. His emotions and imagination run wild. Invariably he becomes a mythomaniac (see "lying").

As usual, all the above mentioned signs do not necessarily have to be present in order to detect psychosis. After examining the samples below and in the last chapter, you should be able to do so effortlessly.

---

sadomasochism
The following three samples belong to regressive personality types: those who exhibit infantile behavior. The last two also display possible psychopathic personalities. Their script is monotonous. These samples belong to student applicants with such monotonous scripts, no other signs are necessary to detect the psychotic personality.

A THEATER WHICH ALSO WAS
THE THEATER FINALLY ALSO
2 MONTHS I LEFT FOR A ME
APPLIED TO HARVARD. I WA
AND ATTENDED HARVARD FOR
QUITTING. I REALLY DISCU

This man of twenty-six has spent many years in psychoanalysis. His low intelligence is apparent by the slow, affected handwriting.

psychopathic personality

This woman of twenty-five has a rather confused mind with manual rather than intellectual creativity.

> IN IRELAND WHERE WE
> WE WERE ALREADY BOOKED.
> WHAT WITH THE BOMBINGS,
> FERRY STRIKES AND THE
> PEPE'S VISIT, FRANCE
> APPEARS CHAOTIC! SORRY
> TO MISS YOUR EXHIBITIONS
> AND THE CHANCE TO VIEW
> YOUR PATUS. WILL CATCH

This young man of twenty-four is on medication. He has a slow mind, little intelligence, and is lazy.

> n out, for days I tried to ring
> out but either my parents had
> liday for a week. Therefore I made
> tion of home which brought me

---

manic-depressive personality

This sample of monotonous writing shows altered and tapered strokes that make it difficult to read. The writer is forty-four years old, a borderline case that could also be categorized as schizophrenic. His anxiety causes him to constantly try to improve his strokes. His destructive tendencies are strong, judging from the odd spacing, angles, and the reversed, tapered strokes. The writer lives in a fantasy world and lies all the time.

Here is a forty-two-year-old man who is highly intelligent. His great agitation causes aphasia. His writing displays a meandering, descendant baseline, light pressure, with altered, retouched letters.

Nancy,

Sorry for the corney card but hard to track you down. Please give me a ~~ring~~ call when you have a chance.

Bill

This is a very confused forty-seven-year-old woman who has tried to commit suicide. She suffers periods of agitation followed by deep depressions during which she cannot move. She has a split and weak personality.

street as to back experience — I can with any body but of mental poverty is my — you honey — what isnt easy —

Her sample shows: Slow, regressive, difficult-to-read writing (confusion, little reasoning and intelligence, problem overcoming the past); heavy "i" dots (psychosis); meandering baseline and light, irregular pressure (instability, fatigue); altered letters (lying, dissimulation, dishonesty); twisted strokes (suffering); odd spacing inside words (schizoid tendencies); thin or broken strokes and "o" in the form of a heart (high blood pressure, anxiety); tapered strokes and stems (destructive tendencies); general incoherence (confusion, deviated emotions).

This is a man of fifty-five who has never held a job for more than a few months. He has changed professions, wives, and life styles over a dozen times each. Periods of agitation alternate with deep depressions.

reflection of lights in the streets reminds me

His writing shows: Light pressure; very meandering baseline; varying slants; altered, imprecise letters that are unfinished and broken; numerous twisted and reversed strokes; various tapered crossings of the letter "t"; heavy "i" dots; descendant end-strokes; generous, irregular spacing; crossed-out signature at the left-hand side. The small and speedy writing illustrates his intelligence and agitation.

---

paranoid personality

This journalist, thirty-eight years old, has been in psychoanalysis for many years. He is very intelligent.

several times but this time it was quite different. I guess that the people who are there matter more and more to me

This sample shows: Small and speedy writing (intelligence, good education, virility); meandering baseline and light pressure (instability); descendant baselines and end-strokes (depression); extremely generous irregular spacing (independence, isolation, indifference); weak and varying stems and loops in the lower zone (regressive libido, infidelity); tapered strokes (destructive tendencies); heavy dots on "i" (psychosis); broken and thin strokes (physical weakness, high blood pressure); altered letters (mental health disorders, dissimulation, lying).

paranoid megalomania

This depressed man of thirty-three has no profession. He has very high aims that he can never achieve. His will power fluctuates and he has low intelligence.

The handwriting shows: Very high upper stems; a meandering baseline; irregular pressure; hooks; coils; regressive angular strokes; altered letters; generous spacing; and heavy "i" dots. The psychotic instability and mythomania are obvious.

We can conclude that it is necessary to proceed cautiously whenever we see handwriting with light pressure and a very meandering baseline. The writer will have serious mental health disorders. He may be highly intelligent and charming; you may be fascinated and hope to be able to help him. This, however, is most likely impossible. His mental illness makes him destructive. Leave such an unstable and potentially dangerous person to the professionals.

Schizophrenia.

The schizophrenic's handwriting is chaotic and not very legible. In these cases it is necessary to read the content. Words or letters might be missing. You may find several languages mixed together in the same sentence. Certain passages may seem completely normal but his behavior is very changeable. Because of his compulsive need to communicate, he will overwhelm you with words and then, suddenly, drop back into muteness.

The schizophrenic lives in a remote, unreal world. Often he has great intelligence and intuition; they enable him to see through you in his search for your weaknesses. (His instability and paranoia lead him to seek to hurt others.) You may find his personality intriguing, but do not try to cure him as an amateur. It is impossible. Medication can temporarily calm a schizophrenic's agitation.

There are three main groups of schizophrenics.

1. *Split personality.* Capital letters or other strokes are disconnected and reversed. Some letters are broken and made with several strokes; a large number of capital letters appear in the middle of words. The same signs seen in the handwriting of psychotics appear in a more pronounced form.

2. *Multiple personality.* Several completely different handwritings on the same page or in messages written at different

times. It is often hard even for a trained graphologist to believe that they were written by the same person.

3. *Schizophrenic criminal.* Usually the pressure is too heavy or too light and the angular script is sometimes extremely monotonous. A large number of signs associated with psychotics are present.

NOTE: Most violent criminals are schizophrenic. Prison cannot rehabilitate them; they need medication. Their libido is weak. The rapist does not have a strong libido; his sexuality is simply deviant. Rape is a crime of violence, not sexual desire.

Needless to say, the schizophrenic is unable to assume a career. He has great difficulty functioning in everyday life because his illness makes him completely irresponsible. He also is callous in regard to other people.

Here are some samples of schizophrenics:

Anorexia and schizophrenia

Here is a woman of twenty-three, a borderline case between psychosis and schizophrenia. The monotonous handwriting shows a regressive personality.

Sexual psychosis

This man of twenty-nine is a rapist. Notice the exaggerated lower loops, the reversed slant, and the monotonous aspect of his handwriting.

This thirty-three year old man is very intelligent and has spent some years in an asylum. His writing includes wide spacings, a regressive slant, and tapered strokes. The inflated loops indicate sexual ambivalence.

Here is a rapist.

Monotonous, pasty writing.

---

split personality

The inflated loops indicate the sexual ambivalence that often appears in the handwriting of the mentally ill.

This handwriting is of an intelligent man of thirty-six who calls himself "The Philosopher." His intuition is highly developed (see the disconnected letters). The sample includes altered strokes of varying pressure. He lives on lithium.

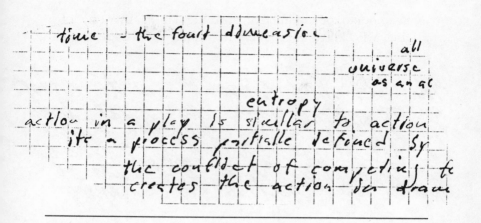

---

schizophrenic criminal
Here is a woman of forty-four.

The monotonous, jumbled, and angular handwriting of a criminal who killed two people for money—and sadistic pleasure.

Murphy has invited us to visit
very much and have just time
if only I could come to Paris
at least something to dream
getting the fires and change
you and Sylvia are happy

Another monotonous handwriting sample from a young man who has spent several months in prison.

Dear Mr. Whitman,

Greetings. I dropped b
with an edition of the Ind
philosophical classic – Bhagava
translated into Russian. It
do well in your Russian seci
If you are interested here
address:

This sample belongs to a violent, potentially criminal, young woman of twenty-four who worked for a short time as a secretary. Twisted and jumbled strokes that launch upward at the end-strokes of some words indicate a bad temper; heavy pressure; a general confused aspect that matches her mind.

SUBSTANCE ABUSE

Alcoholics and chain-smokers.

These addictions often run in families; a child will imitate his parents or other adults in his life. Often the addict has a weak sense of self and can be easily influenced. Many alcoholics and chain-smokers are immature, self-destructive, and suffer from a certain number of mental ailments; the signs from the above-described mental illnesses can, therefore, appear in their handwriting. Frequently, their signature is crossed out by a paraph. Other signs show irregular pressure and clubbed strokes.

When you come across such handwriting you cannot detect the person's affliction with complete certainty. But you will find hints that will lead you to investigate further.

Here are some samples of alcoholics and chain-smokers:

This handwriting belongs to a woman of twenty who has been an alcoholic since her early teens and occasionally smokes hashish. After a time, alcohol and drug abuse affect not only the mental condition but also the physical health of the addict. Let's study this sample in detail:

This morning was rather a strange morning. I had been out in Paris with my friend the night before and we got back to my flat at about 4:30am. We sat in the kitchen and ate bread and then found a bottle of wine and started drinking it.

At about 6:30am I got re-tired and couldn't drink any more wine and we both fell

Her sample has small and speedy writing (intelligence, quick mind); round shapes (femininity); heavy dots on the "i" (psychosis); meandering, descendant baselines (instability, depression); altered and jumbled, reversed strokes (anguish, anxiety); tapered, regressive strokes (destructiveness); light and variable pressure (nerve deficiency); some very thin and broken strokes (bad health, high blood pressure); twisted strokes (suffering).

In spite of her youth, the writer's abuses have already destroyed her mental and physical health. She is confused and cannot put her intelligence to good use.

Drug addicts.

Like the alcoholic, the drug addict has a weak sense of self, little will power, and suffers from various emotional difficulties. This does not imply that he is not intelligent; on the contrary, many drug abusers have a high I.Q. and acute intuition, like schizophrenics, whose handwriting is often similar. This similarity is logical because drugs destroy the addict's emotional health and his nervous system. The drug addict's handwriting becomes reversed, imprecise and monotonous. Not surprisingly, a drug addict can also become an alcoholic, a manic-depressive psychotic, or a schizophrenic criminal. The signs in the handwriting will be the same. It shall be up to you to investigate further when you see the many negative signs in his handwriting. Don't forget that all emotionally plagued people—alcoholics and drug addicts among them—fantasize and lie much of the time. Here some samples of drug addicts follow.

The handwriting of a person who has just started abusing will still be clear and readable. It will, however, have a slightly reversed slant and a monotonous aspect, meaning immaturity and infantilism. The first two samples belong to a recent addict.

Here is a young man of twenty-four. He is a cocaine abuser and occasional dealer.

A young woman of eighteen who smokes marijuana daily.

of cigarettes'
After having cleared up and
fast I begun to feel slightly
then and I ventured out to
for a coffee. The improvement
not last long, and I soon

A man of twenty-five who is a heroin addict and needs daily fixes.

Shakespeare Company
37 Rue de la Bûcherie
Paris, France 5e

This man of twenty-nine is a cocaine addict.

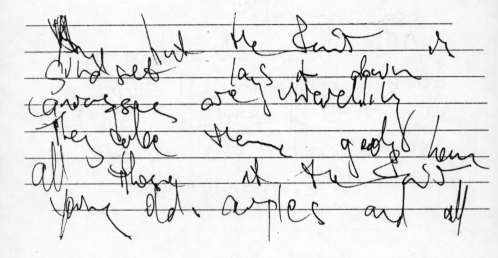

This twenty-seven year old man is a heroin addict, occasional dealer, and violent. He is still in good physical condition as can be seen in the strong and regular pressure of his handwriting. However, his nervous system has already begun to deteriorate. Monotonous aspect and upward launching strokes indicate that he cannot control his temper. He has strong, destructive tendencies.

This heroin addict and dealer is forty-four years old. He is a second-rate jazz musician who tries to give up his habit. His mental state is confused and his will power weak, as can be seen in his exceedingly long horizontal "t" strokes.

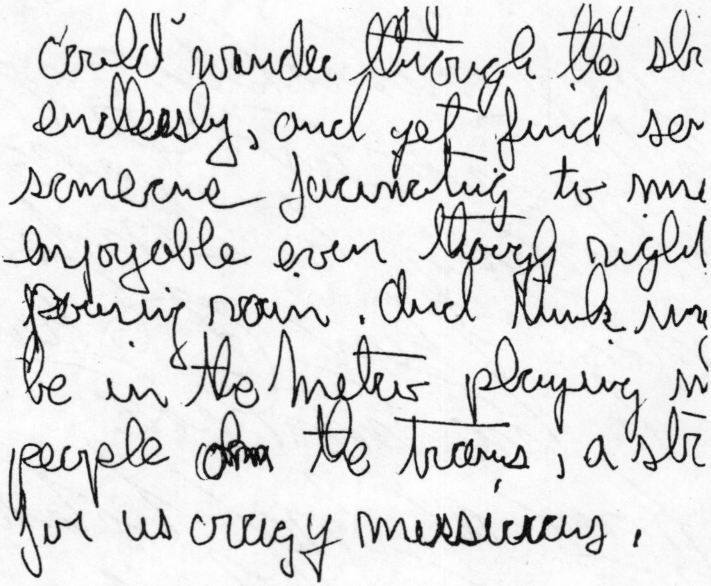

This woman is forty-six years old. She is also an alcoholic and a cocaine addict.

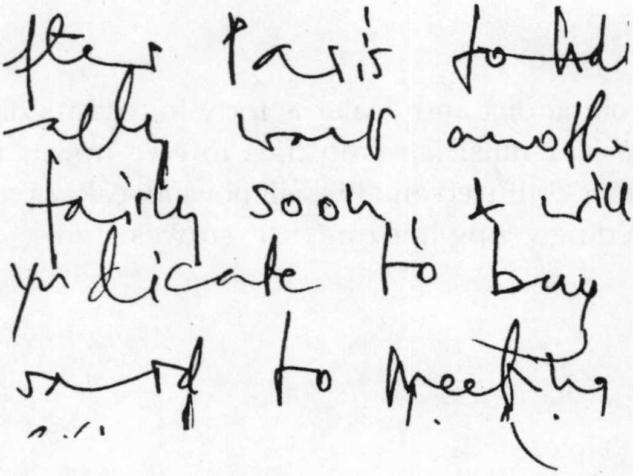

This sample belongs to a teenager who is both a cocaine addict and an alcoholic.

Why are the handwritings of drug addicts similar to those of psychotics or schizophrenics? Are the former trying to escape their mental ailments through drugs? Did they become mentally ill because of their addiction? These questions remain open.

SEXUALITY

In order to build a satisfactory romantic relationship with someone, it is necessary to be sexually compatible. Graphology will help you detect the sexuality of a potential partner. It is best not to choose samples from adolescents, since their sexuality is often not stabilized and is frequently still narcissistic.

Sexuality shows itself in the loops and stems of the lower zone.

Normal sexuality:

Sexual frustration:

Inhibited sexual desire, impotence, indifference:

Sexual ambivalence: Varying slant and clubbed horizontal strokes.

Homosexuality:

Fantasies of debauchery and perversions: Pasty, ink-filled letters.

filed, gone

Sadism:

Repression, neurosis:

Infidelity: Varying shapes and lengths in the lower zone.

unfaithfulness; signe of

Potential rapist: Clubbed, irregular stems.

further, off, g

The snake.

If possible, ask the writer to draw a snake at the end of his sample. Do not give him any more information. His drawing will provide you with some additional indication as to his sexuality, although its analysis is less precise than that of general signs in handwriting.

Male sexuality

strong libido

average libido

weak, regressive libido

very weak, inhibited, and frustrated libido; extreme auto-erotism, which interferes with sexual relationships

no libido; no interest in sex

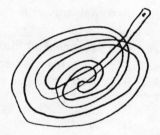

fluctuating libido; homosexual tendencies

Female sexuality

average libido

no libido; no interest in sex

strong libido; possibly homosexual tendencies; fantasy

NOTE: You will notice that only three configurations are given for female sexuality, while six are given for male sexuality. Research has not yet revealed additional configurations for female subjects. (For instance, no specific design for female inhibited and frustrated libido has surfaced yet.)

Free combination.

The following test of drawings will also assist in discovering a person's sexual, manual, or technical and intellectual tendencies.

Show him a triangle, a square, and a circle and ask him to construct a human being with them. No other strokes are allowed. These three symbols can be of any size and repeated as often as he wants.

Meaning:
The triangle represents sexuality

the square represents materialism and technical and manual
   ability

the circle represents the imagination and intellectual ability

See which symbols predominate.

A sensual and sexual person.	A materialistic, manually or technically inclined person.	A sensitive, intellectual person.

3

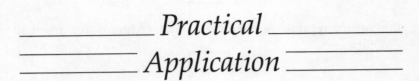

Practical
Application

In handwriting analysis, the interplay and accumulation of various signs together describe a specific character trait. The practical exercises in this chapter will help you make the right choice when several meanings are possible. In general, predominant and frequently recurring signs indicate a specific character trait—a trait more pronounced in him than in most other people. Because you have to examine a large number of samples in order to progress, all the samples in this chapter are new and have not been shown in any other chapters or books.

There are different methods of professional and amateur analysis, depending on the purpose. All methods are based on many years of practical research and application. Choose the method that suits you best; however, try to avoid the mathematical, so-called "grapho-metrical" methods as they give a stereotyped picture of the writer. An analysis made by a computer cannot present a lively, precise portrait. Each person is unique!

To repeat: The profession, age, and sex of the person under analysis must always be known first.

Remember also that the handwriting of renowned artists will

be of little practical use, since their excesses and eccentricities find release in their art. However, just for amusement, you will see samples from a few famous artists and writers at the end of our practical exercises.

If possible, analyze samples written on white unlined paper with a fountain pen or ball point—a black ball point is ideal. In the beginning it will be difficult for you to study samples produced with felt pens; colored pencils must be avoided altogether, as it is impossible to evaluate their pressure.

HANDWRITING SAMPLES

This woman is twenty-four and a literature student.

Dear Claude,
        hi there. Here I am again on desk duty at Shakespeare's. It's about 9 o'clock, and I've just been out for a bite to eat with Christina and her newly arrived friend from Australia, David, and Eric. It looks like being a relatively quiet night in the shop. Bye now Jane.
        Jordan.

Her handwriting shows: Strong, regular pressure (good physical health); normal size and spacing (well-balanced, organized person); slightly meandering baseline (quick mind, intelligence, good education); large right margin (timidity, inhibition); tapered, slightly launching upward, short end-strokes (vulnerability); arcades in some connections (arrogance); round and angular strokes (intelligence); knotted loops (will power, perseverance); knotted loops in the "s": (jealousy, possessiveness); reversed, tapered strokes (destructiveness); coils and covered strokes (diplomacy, dishonesty, business acumen, selfishness); superfluous dots—after the signature—(distrust, lying); progressive slant (dynamism, ambition); connected script (analytical and deductive mind, sociability).

PORTRAIT: The subject is in good physical and mental condition. She is organized, well-balanced, educated, and perseverant. She should succeed in her studies. Her strong will power opens many careers to her—teaching, politics, business, and publicity would be good choices. There is a need to be surrounded by people. An isolated activity, like research, is not in order.

In her private life she is affectionate, sensual, and sexual. She is easy to live with, very friendly and helpful despite her inner selfishness. She tries to hide her arrogance and vulnerability. Her inhibitions will disappear in a few years; at that time she may stop lying, since she does it from anxiety and fear.

We can conclude that her writing is positive overall.

Here is a female student of twenty-four just finishing her Ph.D.

against the light : if the text pressure is heavy . In spite of books cannot yet exemplify our limit ourselves to a few examples

Her handwriting shows: An upward slant (analytical, reasoning mind); speedy to normal speed (intelligence, quick mind, vivacity); regular, strong pressure (good health); connected script (sociability, attachment to friends and family); short end-strokes (selfishness; lack of generosity); (well-balanced personality); regular size and placement in the different zones (good mental health); knotted loops (perseverance); dtrong horizontal "t" crossings (will power, ambition); round and angular shapes (intelligence, good education, good health); slightly meandering baseline (intelligence, education).

PORTRAIT: The writer is very healthy, with an extremely high I.Q. She will succeed without effort in any chosen career. The negative signs are very few. She has a happy disposition, is easy to live with, and is affectionate, sensual, and sexual. Her libido is very strong—unusual in a person with such a high I.Q.

This handwriting belongs to a man of seventy-two who is still very active. He is a former sportsman of international fame; now he is writing his memoirs. He still swims daily in cold water, gives lectures, and travels throughout the world. He had suffered a bad head injury a few years earlier.

_— me, the fellow who soiled
ig in the outdoor pool.
aging that I can stay in your flat
— I would love that. But at this
see any chance yet. Do let me
in England, I would love to take you_

His sample displays: Speedy and small writing (intelligence, virility, good education); short or twisted strokes and loops in the lower zone (weakened libido); medium, slightly irregular pressure (fairly good health, age considered; high "i" dots (imagination, intellectual creativity); irregular, thin and weak "t" crossings (fluctuating will power); round shapes (friendliness, sociability); connected strokes (analytical and deductive mind; sociability); normal spacing and margins (good mental health, well-balanced character); reversed and twisted strokes (physical suffering, dishonesty); concave end-strokes (generosity); altered strokes and letters (anguish, anxiety; lying); pasty strokes and letters filled with ink (ribald fantasies); clear writing and regular spacing (logic, reason, order).

PORTRAIT: His mental and physical health are fairly good, his age considered, in spite of various ailments caused by former injuries. He is very friendly and sociable. Thanks to his diplomacy he can fit in with any social group and is invited everywhere. However, he often regrets that his libido can no longer match his fantasies, and this makes him resentful.

This man is twenty-four and a literature student.

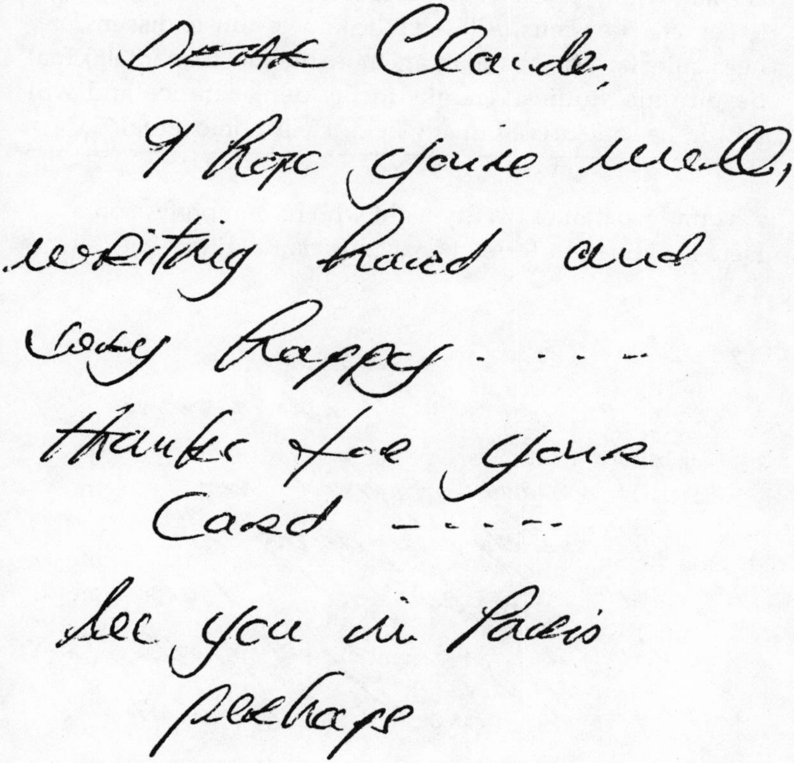

[handwritten note:]

Dear Claude,

I hope you're well,
writing hard and
very happy . . . —
thanks for your
card — . . —

See you in Paris
perhaps

His handwriting shows: strong pressure (good health); large size (charm, "feminine" qualities, manual ability); round garlanded shapes (seductive personality, "feminine" qualities; friendliness); knotted loops (perseverance); regular spacing and clear script (order, honesty, reliability); some capital letters in the middle of words (artistic and manual creativity); strong "t" crossings (will power); coils (business acumen, dissimulation, dishonesty); inflated, open loops, slightly tapered and reversed (homosexuality); connected script (sociability).

PORTRAIT: The young man has much artistic creativity and is in excellent physical and mental health. He works hard and is friendly and sociable. He likes to please and charm people to get what he wants. Although he knows how to dissimulate, he is quite honest. His skills are more manual than intellectual despite his studies. Thanks to his perseverance and will power, he can succeed in any field. He is homosexual.

A young woman of twenty-eight who has no profession. Here is a different form of analyzing handwriting.

Her handwriting displays: Slow, monotonous script; medium pressure; very long loops in the lower zone; high "i" dots; disconnected letters; extremely wide spacing; weak "t" crossings; hooks; straight baseline.

Positive	Negative
clear, orderly mind	inhibition
imagination	sexual frustration
reliability	loneliness
punctuality	neurotic tendencies
good auditory memory	laziness
intuition	greed
ambition	selfishness
business acumen	lack of sensuality
intelligence	unaffectionate nature
fairly good physical health	lack of sociability
independence	parsimony

PORTRAIT: The writer is intelligent but very lonely. She has no set goals and is not very happy in life. Her will power is weak and she has strong neurotic tendencies and chronic depression. She has difficulty living with people and living alone. Her mental sufferings may cause her health to deteriorate.

This man is thirty-two and an engineer.

Here is another form that can be used, especially for professional analysis.

*a. a don't want to see years down the
inated by minimalism or the suburbia/
that have gone blind to the rest of
past thirty years or so, American literature
a impact; the international literary
roete stand justified in their accusations.*

to Europe provide the answer? I would like to be the one to begin he stone obstacle. I once had a dlu, the poetry critic, and she

Intelligence: very good
Education: good
Organization: perfect
Analytical and deductive reasoning: excellent
Decision-making ability: excellent
Initiative: very pronounced
Adaptability: perfect
Flexibility: good
Perseverance: perfect
Ambition: high
Will power: good
Diligence: very high
Pragmatism: perfect
Materialism: good
Imagination: good
Creativity: poor
Intuition: absent
Diplomacy: very good
Attitude towards others: perfectly polite
Business acumen: good
Susceptibility to influence: low
Dynamism: good
Quickness of mind: fairly good
Patience: excellent
Authority: good
Reliability: satisfactory

Honesty: satisfactory
Integrity: satisfactory
Trustworthiness: satisfactory
Vitality: good
Punctuality: very good
Logic: good
Ability to work independently: good
Auditory memory: poor
Visual memory: excellent
Ability to concentrate: perfect
Sense of humor: none
Courage: good
Sociability: good
Spontaneity: good
Inhibitions: low
Neurosis: none
Libido: normal
Physical health: good
Mental health: good

This is a very positive handwriting. The applicant should be hired.

NOTE: The content and the length of this list depends upon the profession and position to be filled.

PROFESSIONAL PORTRAIT: The applicant is intelligent, well-educated, with an analytical and deductive mind. He knows how to organize and assume responsibility. He is punctual and reliable. Perseverant and pragmatic, he achieves his goals. He has strong will power and imagination. Very sociable, he can integrate himself into any working group, and is discreet and diplomatic.

PRIVATE PORTRAIT: The writer is attached to his family and friends. He is affectionate, sensual, and sexual, and is faithful to his wife. His character is well-balanced. However, he is quite jealous, possessive, and selfish. There is a certain lack of humor. He is critical and principled.

This young woman of twenty-six has been a student, a secretary, and a teacher.

— some decisions. (Its alarming to see se days). My spirit really perked up ise w/back pay which amounted to hour which is a salary that I feel Unfortunately I've been informed ng alternate weekends like everybody

ing to start in a training riting to illiterate adults. Its e church that Mark works at.

Her sample shows: Speedy, reversed, disconnected writing; light pressure; unfinished strokes; altered and tapered letters; pronounced upper zone; stick-like stems.

PORTRAIT: Intelligent, well-educated, and very sensitive person with excellent intuition. She is, however, very selfish, immature, and inhibited. She is not very sociable and is extremely stubborn. Her inner sufferings over the past are hidden through lying. Her ambition and her spontaneity are limited; she is vulnerable and not very happy. There are neurotic and destructive tendencies; her acute anxiety induces her to lie much of the time.

HANDWRITING SAMPLES OF
FAMOUS ARTISTS

George Bernard Shaw at eighty-seven.

Slightly meandering baseline (well-balanced and educated person).

Strong pressure (good physical health).

Speedy and connected writing (intelligence, education, quick and analytical mind, good visual memory, sociability).

Small size (intelligence, virility).

High "i" dots and upper stems (imagination, high aims, intellectual creativity).

Strong "t" crossings above the stems (authority, decisiveness, will power).
Straight slant (reason, good concentration).
Regular spacing (clear mind).
Angular script (virility, ambition, dynamism).

PORTRAIT: Despite his advanced age, his mind is still clear, active, and creative. His handwriting shows his above average intelligence. Although a great artist, his character is well-balanced: his ambition and strong will power made possible his great artistic achievement. His mental and physical health are satisfactory. (He died at the age of ninety-four).

Truman Capote at thirty-three.

Very small writing (intelligence).
Speedy writing (quick mind, intelligence, good education).
Strong regular pressure (good health).
Straight baseline (punctuality, will power, organization, reliability).
Slight reversed slant (inhibition, good concentration, diplomacy, dissimulation).
Connected and disconnected writing (analytical mind, intuition, intellectual creativity).

High and heavy "i" dots (imagination, depressive tendencies, neurosis).

Convex, horizontal "t" crossings above the stems (despotism, strong will power).

Pasty letters filled with ink (debauched fantasies).

Very round shapes ("feminine" qualities).

Generous spacing (emotional and intellectual isolation, independence).

This author is well-known to you; draw his portrait with this list of traits.

William Faulkner at thirty-two.

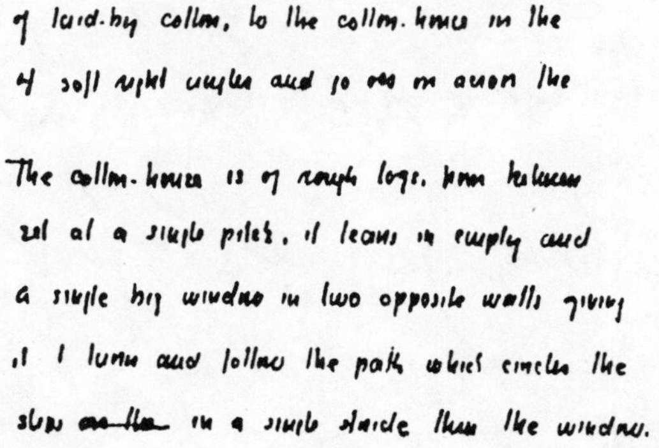

[handwritten text sample]

Speedy and small script (intelligence, quick mind, good education, selfishness, intellectual creativity, virility).

Angular and round shapes (intelligence).

Disconnected script (highly developed intuition, sensitivity, independence).

Regular spacing (clear mind, organization).

Pasty letters filled with ink (imagination, debauched fantasies).

Garlands (friendliness, amiability, adaptability, flexibility).

Straight, slightly progressive slant (sense, reason, ambition, pragmatism).

Straight baseline (will power, punctuality, realism, principles, reliability, honesty).

Monotonous aspect (mental suffering and inhibition). Absence of end-strokes (selfishness, parsimony).

It should be easy for you to synthesize these traits and draw a precise portrait of this literary genius.

Dudley Moore, a contemporary actor, at fifty-two.

The QE2 is not exactly what we bargained for but L.A. will be! O.K.?!!! I love you Brozipozi Dudley x

Speedy and very large writing (spontaneity, ambition, vitality, vanity).

Connected strokes (sociability, attachment to friends and family).

Arcades (arrogance, confidence, manipulation).

Concave initial strokes (sense of humor).

Strong, regular pressure (good physical health).

Reversed angles (vengefulness).

Large, inflated loops in the lower zone (strong libido, fantasies, sexual ambivalence).

Tapered end-strokes launching upward (destructiveness, choleric temper, anger, violence).

Hooks (greed).

Tight "a"s and "o"s (Difficulty overcoming past sufferings and poverty).

Meandering baseline (instability).

Heavy "i" dots (mental ailments, depression).

Knotted loops (perseverance, tenacity, will power).

PORTRAIT: He is in good physical health; however, his mental condition is precarious. He has difficulty overcoming past problems. There are too many contradictions in his rich personality: his generosity, sociability, and attachment to others is counterbalanced, at times, by his destructive tendencies. He is extremely talented, dynamic, and spontaneous, but he has periods of deep depression, during which he needs the help of psychoanalysis. His moods are cyclothymic; his activity can turn into agitation and a sometimes excessive choleric temper. This changeability, as well as a certain arrogance, does not make him easy to live with. The women in his life have to be submissive and adaptable, since he does not like to make many concessions. As a hedonist, he loves the money that buys his pleasures; he can be a showoff and a spendthrift. His genuine generosity, humor, and creativity directly contradict his selfishness, greed, and depressive tendencies. His handwriting illustrates all the complexities that frequently coexist in an artist's character.

"Snakefinger": thirty-seven-year-old male musician; drug addict. Died in 1988, of a heart attack.

> *Breakfast this morning, myself prin ess started on a long day writing. We started by trying to and ended by spitting off the f thing it fall. Altogether a most*

Slow, contrived writing (impaired intelligence due to drug addiction).

Very irregular pressure (poor health).

Unfinished, altered strokes and letters (vulnerability, lying).

Covered strokes (dissimulation, lying, dishonesty).

High stems in the upper zone (mysticism, ambitions beyond his capabilities; vanity).

Inflated, open loops in the lower zone (homosexual tendencies).

Straight and reversed slant and strokes (lying, inhibition, stubbornness).

Stick-like stems (stubbornness, idealism).

Very meandering baseline (instability).

Heavy clubbed strokes (sexual ambivalence, alcohol or drug addiction, deviated emotions).

Broken strokes (high blood pressure, cardiovascular problems).

PORTRAIT: This man is in poor physical and mental health. His prolonged drug abuse has undermined his health. He is confused. The contradictions in his character are too pronounced. His addiction and weak libido make him unhappy. He suffers great anxiety and frustration in his professional life and private life.

Poet Joseph Michael Connors, fifty-two years old.

Strong but irregular pressure (instability, fluctuating will power, precarious health).

Meandering baseline (instability).

Altered letters (dissimulation, lying).

Progressive slant (ambition, spontaneity, passion for work).

Arcades (manipulation, arrogance).

Unfinished strokes (diplomacy, vulnerability).

High upper stems (ideals, ambitions, mysticism).

Speedy writing (quick mind, intelligence).

Coils and reversed strokes (selfishness, business acumen).

Connected script (sociability).

Loops (good concentration).

Narrow "a"s and "o"s (suffering caused by poverty).

Concave "t" crossings (sense of humor).

Signature difficult to read (lying).

High dots on the "i" (imagination).

Altered letters (anxiety, fear-induced lying).

Tapered strokes (destructiveness).

Open stems and loops in the lower zone (weak, unsatisfactory libido).

PORTRAIT: The writer is intelligent, with some creative ability. His goals are high. Despite his sense of humor and imagination, his fluctuating will power (weak "t" crossings) makes it difficult for him to achieve his goals. His whole personality is unstable. He suffers anguish and anxiety that he conceals through lying.

At times he seeks relief in alcohol, and his health is poor. His writing saves him from drowning in confusion.

NOTE: Permission to publish the above handwritings of famous artists has been granted.

SAMPLE TESTS

Try not to cheat by looking through previous chapters or the glossary! But even if you cannot help yourself this exercise will help you strengthen your memory. Most test samples have not appeared elsewhere. Solutions are provided at the end of each section.

General character traits.

Each sample reveals only one of three specific character traits suggested. Which is the correct attribute?

1.
    a) ☐ honesty

    b) ☐ dishonesty

    c) ☐ diplomacy (relatively honest)

help in the future, say the word.

2.
    a) ☐ strong will power

    b) ☐ weak will power

    c) ☐ fluctuating will power

write a little my birthplace

3.
    a) ☐ optimism
    b) ☐ pessimism
    c) ☐ well-balanced outlook

me more what you've done U.S.

4.
    a) ☐ low intelligence
    b) ☐ average intelligence
    c) ☐ exceptional intelligence

particularly lucrative living in Paris being

5.
    a) ☐ spontaneity
    b) ☐ inhibition
    c) ☐ reason

for all good men & to the aid of their

6.
    a) ☐ bad temper, anger

    b) ☐ erudition, courtesy

    c) ☐ timidity, anguish

Mike sends thanks books. Xmas greetings

7.
    a) ☐ mythomania

    b) ☐ imagination

    c) ☐ destructive tendencies

the circle), then I and you're back started.

8.
    a) ☐ analytical mind

    b) ☐ intuition

    c) ☐ manual creativity

Intelligence

9.

a) ☐ greed

b) ☐ thievery

c) ☐ reliability

challengeng from many of view. However!

10.

a) ☐ humor

b) ☐ moodiness

c) ☐ stability

Ice Follies reunion very pleased you c

11.

a) ☐ maturity

b) ☐ immaturity

c) ☐ infantilism, neurosis

many tourists, so we are going to south - France, Bretagne and perhaps Paris again. We hope so, we have to think, about our ! Have a good summer. Best,

12.   a) ☐ stubbornness

                                  b) ☐ openness, adaptability

                                  c) ☐ distrust, lying person

me that you're
no longer work

The solutions follow and are explained in detail. Study them before continuing to the second group of tests.

Solutions:

1. a) Straight baseline; regular pressure, slant, and size; easy-to-read handwriting.
2. b) Varying, light horizontal "t" crossings.
3. c) Regular size and pressure; straight baseline.
4. b) Rather small, speedy, and clear writing.
5. a) Progressive slant.
6. c) Reversed slant; slow and altered writing.
7. c) Tapered and angular strokes.
8. a) Connected script; "i" dots connected to the following letter.
9. b) Hooks, tapered reversed strokes and loops; arcades; coils; angles; altered letters.
10. c) Regular pressure; clear handwriting; straight baseline.
11. b) Schoolish, slow writing; reversed slant.
12. b) Round and angular shapes; speedy and regular writing.

Count 5 points for each correct answer.

> 45–60 = excellent
> 30–45 = good
> 20–30 = average
> 0–20 = read the book again

1.

    a) ☐ punctuality

    b) ☐ reliability

    c) ☐ laziness

October

2.

    a) ☐ dynamism

    b) ☐ ambition

    c) ☐ confusion

I hope you guests like th Sincerely,

3.
    a) ☐ organization

    b) ☐ analytical and
          deductive mind

    c) ☐ materialism

very easy as
inappropriate angle

4.
    a) ☐ tenacity, perseverance

    b) ☐ instability

    c) ☐ impaired will power

my own inner vor
suspecting it to be a
and sure of the fact

5.
    a) ☐ honesty

    b) ☐ dishonesty

    c) ☐ stubbornness

Things are
the research

6.
    a) ☐ inhibition, indecisiveness

    b) ☐ strong will power

    c) ☐ intellectual ability

Black must give up the centre gives White a long-lasting

7.
    a) ☐ independence

    b) ☐ inability to work independently

    c) ☐ indolence, fatigue

The formidable Mr new found frien example to us a

8.
    a) ☐ diligence

    b) ☐ laziness

    c) ☐ good health

Stopped by to

9.
   a) ☐ very critical mind
   b) ☐ impatience
   c) ☐ spontaneity

Because I seem to have

10.
   a) ☐ optimism
   b) ☐ pessimism
   c) ☐ passion for work

Perj.

11.
   a) ☐ hypocrisy
   b) ☐ loyalty
   c) ☐ greed

Village Voice

12.
   a) ☐ anger
   b) ☐ vengefulness
   c) ☐ friendliness, sociability

for your

Solutions:

1. c) Slow, round, and schoolish handwriting.
2. c) Confused handwriting.
3. b) Speedy, small, connected script.
4. c) Weak horizontal "t" crossings; slow writing; weak pressure.
5. c) Reversed slant.
6. b) Short, strong horizontal "t" crossings.
7. b) Tight connections and spaces.
8. c) Strong pressure; clear, easy-to-read handwriting.
9. b) Small, speedy, and imprecise writing; light pressure.
10. b) Descendant baseline; superfluous dots.
11. c) Hooks and coils.
12. a) Tapered, launching upward end-strokes.

Count 5 points for each correct answer.

$$45–60 = \text{excellent}$$
$$30–45 = \text{good}$$
$$20–30 = \text{average}$$
$$0–20 = \text{read the book again}$$

1.

a) ☐ vanity

b) ☐ imagination

c) ☐ manual ability

travels, or whatever

2.
a) ☐ nastiness
b) ☐ friendliness
c) ☐ vengefulness

Sincerely

3.
a) ☐ rectitude
b) ☐ dishonesty
c) ☐ violent tendencies

one should master the

4.
a) ☐ loyalty
b) ☐ slanderous nature
c) ☐ discretion

if you could
i'd really

5.

a) ☐ sociability

b) ☐ isolation, loneliness

c) ☐ cynicism

the rest of my life. I

6.

a) ☐ humor

b) ☐ gravity

c) ☐ joy in living, youthful enthusiasm

to say school was

7.

a) ☐ mathematical skill

b) ☐ poetic talent

c) ☐ manual or athletic ability

which I long entangled?

8.

   a) ☐ good concentration

   b) ☐ poor concentration

   c) ☐ confusion

and I find graphology

9.

   a) ☐ good visual memory

   b) ☐ good auditory memory

   c) ☐ poor memory

Green Island on the Great Barrier Reef - went swimming in water 28°Celsius & watched the fishes through glassbottom boats

---

10.

   a) ☐ good adaptability and group integration

   b) ☐ inhibition, poor communication

   c) ☐ manipulation

compagny

11.

a) ☐ business acumen

b) ☐ management ability

c) ☐ craftsmanship

finds

12.

a) ☐ diligence

b) ☐ laziness

c) ☐ sporadic courage

*try to join J-C. Lemagny
calling the upper million*

Solutions:

Count 5 points for each correct answer.

1. a) Excessively high stems.
2. b) Round shapes; regular pressure and strokes; garlands.
3. a) Very regular, sometimes stick-like handwriting.
4. b) Large, imprecise writing; progressive slant.
5. b) Very generous spacing; upward slant; reversed strokes.
6. c) Speedy, progressive writing.
7. c) Slow writing; heavy regular pressure; script mainly in the middle and lower zones.
8. a) Upward slant; backward strokes; knotted loops.
9. b) Disconnected, slow, and regular writing.
10. c) Arcades; slow, reversed script with hooks.
11. c) Script mainly in the lower zone; slow writing.

12. c) Weak horizontal "t" crossings.

$$45–60 = \text{excellent}$$
$$35–45 = \text{good}$$
$$20–35 = \text{average}$$
$$0–20 = \text{read the book again}$$

Adolescent development and aptitude.

In this series the samples are fewer but longer; they all belong to young people between fifteen and eighteen years of age. When you analyze adolescent handwritings make many more allowances than with adult handwriting, because their characters are still unformed. Before the age of twenty-four personality can change from one day to another.

1.

a) ☐ advanced study of literature or history

b) ☐ technical study

c) ☐ business career or study

Dear Claude

How is New-York?

School was great today! I finally feel that after the "Alliance" I went to a café wit Unfortunately we spoke English all the time a chance to practice my French.

The metro people are still on strike, everyone up ; causing inconvience, to all, that all will be back to normal soon.

yours sincerely

Mercy

2.

   a) ☐ artistic career: acting, painting, decorating; no advanced study

   b) ☐ active life: travel, social contacts

   c) ☐ intellectual career: study, research, teaching

got this radio play

rned out strange. I'd

ple take a look at

3.

a) ☐ mathematics:
computers, accounting,
stock market

b) ☐ training and executive
career

c) ☐ law or economics

sessions at night and sellin
of Dublin scenes — Trinity C̃
O'connell Bridge etc. The D̃
are nothing compared to the
noble buildings of Paris but
their own personal beauty.

4.

a) ☐ talented craftsman

b) ☐ sporting activity: athlete, organizer, trainer

c) ☐ independent business person without special preparatory study (salesperson or small store owner)

Maybe just reading about flowing under-ground water will be cooling.

Solutions:

1. a) Strong, regular pressure and strokes; good spacing; the writing of this sixteen-year-old is clear, well-ordered, with a straight baseline and slant. Pronounced upper zone reveals high ambition, good concentration, and perseverance. His writing is remarkably stable for his age.
2. a) Strong pressure; large, regular, and slow writing; stick-like strokes; knotted loops; short, heavy "t" crossings. The writer has manual and artistic creativity. He requires movement and physical exercise. His strong will power and hard-working temperament allow him to achieve his goals.
3. a) Strong, regular pressure; slight backward slant; regular size and shape; knotted loops; straight baseline.
4. c) Regular writing and pressure; coils, hooks, knotted loops; straight baseline; "t" crossings with a connected loop above the stem (strong will power and authority); script mainly in the middle zone; normal to generous spacing (independence).

Count 10 points for each correct answer.

$$30–40 = \text{excellent}$$
$$20–30 = \text{good}$$
$$10–20 = \text{average}$$
$$0–20 = \text{read the book again}$$

Physical and mental health.

This section is slightly more difficult; be satisfied with even a few correct answers.

1.

   a) ☐ good health

   b) ☐ precarious mental
       health

   c) ☐ precarious physical
       health

teenagers, the backward slant
berty . As regards lefthanders
You may argue that concen-
the writer is self - centred

2.

   a) ☐ psychosis

   b) ☐ chronic neurosis

   c) ☐ schizophrenia

from here forth with
to find a whore
who does not sleep
upon the floor.

3.

a) ☐ good physical and precarious mental health

b) ☐ good mental health; weak physical condition

c) ☐ manic-depression and weak physical condition

about not getting
-s at the hotel →
one woman there who
helpful not all with

4.

a) ☐ stomach ulcers

b) ☐ thyroid disorders

c) ☐ high blood pressure

Kenilworth Road

5.

a) ☐ psychosis

b) ☐ slight, reactional depression

c) ☐ schizophrenia with violent and destructive tendencies.

[handwriting sample: "A WOMAN WHO LIFE AN TO"]

6.

a) ☐ Alzheimer's disease

b) ☐ anxiety, infantilism

c) ☐ good physical and mental health

[handwriting sample: "BUT THEN, QUITE BENNINGTON AND F WAS ACCEPTED, AND WONDERFUL INSTIT"]

7.

a) ☐ confusion

b) ☐ dishonesty

c) ☐ mythomania

Previous to that, the (my birth marked the begin for it!) Father can boast actor, stand-u rugby player, would-be

8.

a) ☐ hysteric

b) ☐ suicidal tendencies

c) ☐ general violent and destructive tendencies

HAVE BETWEEN EACH WORLD I'VE BEEN EUROPE. BY BICYCLE AM MOVING TOWARDS & BACK TO. ZIMBA

9.

a) ☐ inhibition, anguish

b) ☐ megalomania

c) ☐ very high I.Q.; extreme instability; cyclothymia

landscape were good, the talks
dreadful. It was aimed at
to German relations, but my
clearly worsened them!.
mg your mail into a single
expressing it in case it is

10.

a) ☐ high blood pressure

b) ☐ general cardiovascular problems

c) ☐ anorexia

.or, Mercedes, Darren, Lyndon,
Mateus, Geoff, Baskerville, THE
times, I'm glad I wasn't
You've all welcome down

11.

    a) ☐ instability

    b) ☐ good health, stability

    c) ☐ good physical health;
           regression; infantilism

what wonders await you
I am newly re-arrived
in this quiet epistolary

12.

    a) ☐ good mental and
           physical health

    b) ☐ schizophrenia

    c) ☐ chronic neurosis

Taken in Minnea.
names are on the
the picture.
sends her best

Solutions:

1. a) Strong, regular pressure; regular spacing; clear hand-writing.
2. a) Reversed slant and strokes; arcades; confused, irregular spacing; letter "o" written clockwise.
3. b) Speedy, regular, and clear handwriting; weak pressure; broken and twisted strokes.
4. b) Twisted, reversed strokes and letters.
5. c) Confused handwriting; reversed, angular, and tapered strokes; altered letters.
6. b) Reversed slant; monotonous script; altered letters; over-lapping strokes.
7. c) Reversed strokes; overlapping, unfinished, altered letters; irregular pressure; confused handwriting; irregular speed, superfluous dots, arcades (nine signs of lying).
8. a) Speedy, tapered, and confused strokes.
9. c) Speedy, and small writing; meandering baseline. Altered letters; unfinished strokes; heavy "i" dots.
10. c) Slow, monotonous, schoolish handwriting; slight back-ward slant; altered letters.
11. a) Meandering baseline; irregular pressure; tapered and al-tered strokes.
12. a) Clear, regular handwriting; strong pressure.

Remember, this test is not easy; 15 or 20 points mean progress. Count 5 points for each correct answer.

$$40–60 = \text{excellent}$$
$$20–40 = \text{good}$$
$$10–20 = \text{average}$$
$$0–10 = \text{read the book again}$$

Substance Abuse.

Like the physical and mental health test, this test is difficult because many of the signs of mental and physical health problems can be found in the handwriting of substance abusers, and vice versa. Alcohol and drugs affect the physical and the mental condition after prolonged abuse; also, many mentally ill people seek relief through drugs.

1.

    a) ☐ alcoholic

    b) ☐ hard drug addict

    c) ☐ beginning marijuana
       smoker

u I'm finally leau en route to Austr London, so I was h might be able to eome

2.
   a) ☐ alcoholic; physically and mentally ill person

   b) ☐ violent heroin addict

   c) ☐ young drug dealer

I spent practically time in bed, it of my head. Now

3.
   a) ☐ older, long-time drug addict

   b) ☐ psychopath; drug and alcohol abuser; physical and mental disorders

   c) ☐ schizophrenia; drug abuse

and I didnt climb through to the translatin problems.

4.
a) ☐ manic-depressive youth seeking escape in drugs (cocaine); physical condition still good

b) ☐ relatively young person on hard drugs for many years; bad health

c) ☐ violent alcoholic

~ (əl)

that for example in chess

,lay does not express their

body may play a very

5.
a) ☐ young drug dealer and addict; mental and physical ailments

b) ☐ middle-aged man; manic-depressive drug addict

c) ☐ unstable drug addict; homosexual

find myself a frustrated

the novel again, talting

elegant lady, who for some

6.
    a) ☐ no alcohol or drug abuse

    b) ☐ drug addict

    c) ☐ alcoholic

-erred ʹ. CourT's ThaT I
The Correcm and ThaT
o I WiLL NoT ˎfacility
ᴠ CorrecTioNal fa. ᶜfered

Solutions:

This series is difficult and your score will be low. The following explanations will help your progress. Count 10 points for each correct answer.

1. c) Altered letters and strokes (anxiety); reversed, tapered open loops in the lower zone (self-destructive tendencies); slow, monotonous writing; descendant baselines and end-strokes (depression).
2. b) Self-explanatory.
3. b) Hooks; coils; slow, monotonous writing; twisted, altered letters; reversed, tapered, open loops in a rounded handwriting (self-destructive tendencies and sexual ambivalence).
4. a) Monotonous schoolish writing; regular pressure.
5. b) Altered and twisted letters; irregular pressure and slant; hooks; tapered, reversed, and angular strokes; heavy "i" dots; meandering baseline.

6. b) Slow, contrived, monotonous, and confused handwriting (a violent drug addict in prison for life, for murder).

$$40\text{--}60 = \text{excellent}$$
$$10\text{--}40 = \text{good}$$

Finding the "ideal" romantic partner (if such a partner exists).

1.
    a) ☐ sensuality

    b) ☐ affection

    c) ☐ strong libido

stay until

2.
    a) ☐ strong libido

    b) ☐ weak libido

    c) ☐ no libido

possible it would

3.

a) ☐ very feminine
   personality

b) ☐ very masculine
   personality

c) ☐ well-balanced
   personality with a
   strong libido

I think of you so

4.

a) ☐ charm, seduction

b) ☐ toughness, aggression

c) ☐ inhibition, isolation

*might have something to do
with it. Hope everything's
going well at your end.*

5.

a) ☐ generosity

b) ☐ extravagance

c) ☐ avariciousness

*Very little news.
Perseverance brings
good fortune to the
wanderer. I see your
friends from time to*

6.
a) ☐ sensitivity, romance

b) ☐ intuition

c) ☐ coldness, selfishness

you visit

7.
a) ☐ fidelity

b) ☐ debauchery

c) ☐ instability, infidelity

things to do and go jogging in reservoir - yw

8.
a) ☐ honesty

b) ☐ dishonesty

c) ☐ greed

registering for

9.

a) ☐ vulnerability

b) ☐ joy in living

c) ☐ vengefulness

eat, but cl think

10.

a) ☐ spontaneity

b) ☐ inhibition, poor communication

c) ☐ elusiveness

her kunn he

11.

a) ☐ sociability

b) ☐ independence

c) ☐ introversion

Instead I covered mee he connected the

12.

a) ☐ tolerance, complaisance

b) ☐ principled, hard-to-please person

c) ☐ aloof, indifferent person

and interest

NOTE: An affectionate person enjoys kissing; a sexual person enjoys the act of sex; a sensual person is sensitive to the total experience of the body and towards his or her partner's needs. All three are necessary for a strong libido.

Solutions:

1. c) Strong pressure; long, closed loops in the lower zone.
2. b) Weak pressure; weak, tapered vertical strokes hanging in the lower zone.
3. a) Rounded shapes.
4. c) Tight, slow writing; extremely generous spacing.
5. c) Small and tight handwriting.
6. b) Light pressure; speedy, disconnected script.
7. c) Meandering baseline; large variety of shapes and lengths in the lower zone.
8. c) Reversed, angular strokes; jumbled writing; hooks; coils.
9. a) Light pressure; slightly upturned, tapered end-strokes.
10. c) Speedy, imprecise, thread-like script.
11. a) Connected strokes; strong pressure; regular size and spacing.
12. b) Strong, regular pressure; stick-like, regular shapes; arcades; straight baseline.

$$45–60 = \text{excellent}$$
$$30–45 = \text{good}$$
$$20–30 = \text{average}$$
$$0–20 = \text{read the book again}$$

Intimate character traits.

This last test shows that you can see some important character traits by examining only one or two words; sometimes this is all you can obtain.

1.
a) ☐ friendliness, sociability
b) ☐ slanderous nature
c) ☐ discretion

Warmest personal regards from a special friend

2.
a) ☐ jealousy, possessiveness
b) ☐ despotism
c) ☐ indifference

sparkling

3.
a) ☐ anger, bad temper
b) ☐ arrogance
c) ☐ courtesy

student of his pleased

---

4. man's handwriting

a) ☐ hedonism

b) ☐ depressive tendencies

c) ☐ sexual ambivalence

much for listening

5.

a) ☐ strong libido

b) ☐ weak libido

c) ☐ no libido

jumping

6.

a) ☐ humor

b) ☐ egocentrism

c) ☐ destructiveness

now but I miss his
commemorative building

---

7. woman's handwriting

    a) ☐ ambivalence towards femininity

    b) ☐ passion, ambition

    c) ☐ fatigue, laziness

enjoy my duck.
for lunch and is

---

8. man's handwriting

    a) ☐ homosexual tendencies

    b) ☐ bisexual tendencies

    c) ☐ heterosexual tendencies

All my love.

---

9. woman's handwriting

    a) ☐ homosexuality

    b) ☐ bisexuality

    c) ☐ heterosexuality

but it is uncertain if they
will arrive. they are:

10.

a) ☐ intelligence, quick mind

b) ☐ low intelligence, little education

c) ☐ manual creativity

I talked

11.

a) ☐ adaptability

b) ☐ selfishness

c) ☐ stubborness

In absolutely, desperate for a bicycle... but you've

12.

a) ☐ sportsperson

b) ☐ intellectual

c) ☐ dreamer, poet

forward to at the Ice

Solutions:

1. c) Upward and slightly regressive slant; reversed angles and strokes; strong pressure; tight, connected script.
2. a) Knotted loop in "s".
3. b) Arcades in connecting strokes.
4. c) Clubbed, horizontal end-strokes; inflated loops in the lower zone; rounded shapes.
5. a) Long, closed loops in the lower zone.
6. b) Tight, reversed script.
7. b) Extremely progressive slant in a small and speedy writing.
8. a) Rounded shapes; inflated, reversed, open loops in the lower zone.
9. a) Speedy, angular script.
10. b) Large, embellished, slow, and jumbled script.
11. b) Tight, angular and tapered strokes.
12. a) Strong pressure; slow writing; script mainly in the medium and lower zones; long loops falling into lines below.

Count 5 points for each correct answer.

45–60 = excellent
30–45 = good
20–30 = average
  0–20 = read the book again

CONCLUSION

Any novice who has studied this book carefully is now capable of analyzing the handwriting of his friends or acquaintances. He will discover what they think and how they behave. Are they honest and reliable? Are they in good health? Have they a strong libido? And so forth. Psychology and lie-detectors can provide only general information. As we have seen, graphology can show you the precise details of a person's behavior in daily life.